Slanted Justice

By
Zed Wondemu

Dedications

I dedicate this book to my late husband, Dr. Basliel W. Gabriel, who gave me complete freedom and support to excel and focus on my work without any destruction. He was a very unique individual with so many talents and intellect. An amazing and extraordinary father to our beloved children. He was indeed a noble person, with high integrity and patience. May He Rest in Peace. I know he is at peace in heaven.

Foreword

This is not the America I once knew.

America used to be a beacon of hope: a land of freedom, boundless opportunity, and unwavering motivation. Hard work and the pursuit of financial independence were celebrated as noble ambitions. But now, it seems the mantra has shifted from working hard to working smart—even if it means disregarding others to get ahead based on greed, selfishness, and power grab.

What has changed in our nation? Who is responsible for diminishing the values that once made America so admired? This country, which once stood as an inspiration to the world, is now grappling with division and discord. Nations worldwide still aspire to America's ideals, while we seem to be stepping away from the very principles they admire. Individuals and families sacrifice their homeland to come to the USA for freedom, liberty, and justice.

Justice in America is very close to its definition more than any other country. True justice is a concept that transcends simple legality or punishment; it is the pursuit of fairness, equity, and moral rightness in human relationships and systems. It aligns with giving each individual what they are due, whether accountability for crimes, protection of rights, or equal opportunities and fairness.

True justice is understood through key principles:

True justice ensures impartial and unbiased decisions and actions. It treats individuals equally, regardless of status, race, gender, or other socioeconomic characteristics.

True justice ensures that systems and resources are adjusted to address those differences, creating genuine opportunities for all. While fairness often emphasizes equality, equity acknowledges that different people have different needs and status quo.

True justice requires that actions have consequences. Individuals who harm others or society should be held accountable, but in a way that is proportionate, rehabilitative, and aimed at preventing future harm.

True justice seeks to remedy the harm to victims, communities, and even offenders beyond punishment. It emphasizes healing and reconciliation rather than perpetuating cycles of revenge.

True justice upholds the integral worth of every individual. It means even when an individual has committed a wrong, they should be treated with humanity and offered the chance for redemption.

True justice is not limited to individuals; it also addresses systemic inequalities. It seeks to dismantle structures that promote oppression and ensure everyone has access to the same rights, resources, and opportunities. Justice without equality is like an empty vessel.

True justice aligns with ethical principles that transcend written laws. Sometimes, laws can be unjust, and true justice requires questioning and challenging them when they contradict fundamental human rights and values.

True justice is dynamic and compassionate at its heart, rooted in the understanding that human beings are interconnected. It strives not entirely for punishment or legal conformity, but for a world where all individuals can live with dignity, freedom, and fairness.

Immigration has always been America's strength. Embracing diversity and welcoming people from every corner of the world—this was once a source of pride. Yet, we seem to have forgotten the need to impart our democratic principles, respect for human rights, and core values to those who arrive. Instead, we risk creating confusion, where differing customs and practices clash rather than blend. What should be a beautiful exchange of cultures and ideals can sometimes foster misunderstanding and tension. America benefited from immigrants by tapping their labor, talents, and brain power. Immigrants come to this country hungry for work and hungry for education and opportunity. They give it their best to produce, innovate, and contribute with love and loyalty.

At its best, cultural exchange creates understanding, builds respect, and nurtures compassion. It promotes tolerance, love, and peace—the very essence of a civilized society. So, I ask: what do we gain by allowing division and hate to take root in a land that once symbolized unity and progress? Destruction, greed, and animosity only bring us loss, creating a society plagued by fear and distrust. Why are we stifling our progress? Why have we allowed these forces to creep into the heart of our nation?

Isn't it our duty to teach the next generation values of hope, creativity, and compassion? Are we showing them the importance of family, community, and respect, or are we unintentionally endorsing selfishness and power? In our schools, are we encouraging curiosity, kindness, and integrity, or are we allowing harmful influences to shape our children's lives? These harmful influences weaken society at its core. The question is why? Why are we doing this to our children? In turn, this weakened our nation's leadership ability in the areas of commerce, science, and military.

America was once known for standing up for truth and justice. Now, it feels as though the fear of losing security has stifled our willingness to do what's right. I hope that we can revive the spirit of courage, empathy, and resilience that once defined us and that we can pass these ideals on to future generations with renewed pride and conviction for the sake of this country's strength. Strength - financially, spiritually, and militarily. We are leaders, not followers; we are inventors, not copiers.

Contents

Introduction

I was born in Ethiopia to wonderful parents who showered me with love and gave me an incredible life foundation. They spoiled me in the best way possible by sending me to a private boarding school and raising me in an Orthodox Christian home where culture, etiquette, and love were deeply instilled. My upbringing was rich with Ethiopian traditions, from the vibrant food to the profoundly spiritual religious practices, all uniquely Ethiopian. These traditions weren't just things I observed but lessons I lived and embraced, equipping me with pride in my heritage.

This upbringing also taught me the importance of respecting others, following rules, and living a life grounded in decency. Respect and family values are woven into the very fabric of who I am. My parents trusted me implicitly, a trust that profoundly shaped my character. They instilled a strong sense of accountability—I worked tirelessly to preserve their faith in me, and I carry that commitment to this day.

My parents' encouragement and unwavering confidence in me gave me the courage to face challenges head-on and strive for excellence. They believed in my ability to overcome any difficulty, and that belief became the driving force behind my efforts to grow and improve. The trust and love they poured into me didn't just shape my character; they motivated me to constantly aim for something more splendid, always striving to improve.

It felt as though my parents had always known my destiny. When I asked my father if I could go to England for my education, following in the footsteps of my friends, he didn't hesitate. Back then, sending children abroad for education was seen as a mark of prestige. With his blessing, I obtained an F-1 student visa and went to England.

But life there was not what I had imagined. The English education system felt foreign and unfamiliar to me, as I was educated by American teachers. I struggled to adapt. Feeling out of place, I sent a telegram to my father, a heartfelt plea for a ticket and money to join the American education system by coming to the USA. I knew so well. True to his unwavering support, he responded without hesitation.

When I arrived in the United States in 1969, I lived in the basement of an American family's home in Seabrook/Lanham, Maryland, arranged by an Ethiopian friend I'd met in England who had moved here before me. I paid $40.00 monthly for the basement room – a fantastic price. This experience not only eased my transition but also gave me an intimate glimpse into American culture, a glimpse I continue to cherish. I learned to enjoy the taste of shoofly pie, and pumpkin pie for Thanksgiving and Christmas. My only regret is that I did not take the time to learn how to prepare desserts like the shoofly pie.

I enrolled at DuVal High School, where my father, once again, ensured I had everything I needed. He sent money from Ethiopia through Citi Bank to cover all my expenses including college costs and living necessities.

Graduating from high school was a turning point. Without consulting me, my high school counselor decided on Bowie State College for my next step. At first, I was unhappy because I wasn't involved in the decision but quickly realized it was the right decision.

Looking back, I'm deeply grateful for that choice. At Bowie State, I was surrounded by counselors, professors, and classmates who treated me with kindness, respect, and care. Their unwavering support became the cornerstone of my journey, shaping the person I am today.

I came to America with a clear goal: to study, gain knowledge, and eventually return to my homeland. For most of us who traveled from Ethiopia back then, staying in the United States was never part of the plan. We were bound to our roots and only intended to take with us an education that could uplift our communities back home.

After graduating with my undergraduate degree, I initially planned to return to my home country. However, those plans were abruptly upended when the Ethiopian government system shifted dramatically to a socialist military regime. The political turmoil left me stranded. Unable to work due to the restrictions of my student visa, I was overwhelmed with anxiety. In a moment of courage, I decided to visit the office of the Bowie State University President to share my predicament and seek help.

Dr. Samuel L. Myers, the then-president, a man well-versed in global affairs, quickly grasped the gravity of my situation. He asked why I had come, and I shared my story, explaining how the upheaval back home had derailed my return and left me desperate for a job. Humbly, I asked for his assistance.

To my astonishment, he responded with remarkable kindness and compassion—qualities I had come to associate with Bowie State. He told me to return to his office in a month.

When I returned as instructed, I could hardly believe what I heard. The president informed me that he had created a position for me in his office. I was speechless with gratitude. Not only had he extended his lifeline, but the job itself was extraordinary. My role was to read and analyze various newspapers and news clippings based on specific guidelines. This wasn't just employment—it was an education opportunity. I was getting paid to read and enriched my intellectual caliber.

Working in the president's office provided numerous benefits, including learning office protocols, work ethics, and administrative procedures. I also gained invaluable insights from the president, particularly observing his leadership style, communication skills, and eloquent use of language, enriched with a sophisticated vocabulary. In addition, working for the college gave me the entitlement to free graduate school, and I took advantage of the free education and graduated. I earned an MA in education. Upon graduation, my church pastor came to the picture of involving himself in my higher education venture.

My pastor and his wife encouraged me to consider Andrews University for a PhD program. Andrews, a small yet distinguished private university on a picturesque suburban campus in Berrien Springs, Michigan, seemed a promising choice. They graciously drove me there to help me understand the school. My friend's dream did not come true; regardless of their effort and encouragement, I forced myself not to go for the PhD program.

During my visit, I met an Ethiopian lady who was a student at Andrews. She took it upon herself to showcase the campus and its surroundings, painting an inviting picture of life there. As my visit ended, she suggested I meet her brother, who had recently moved from Kentucky to Washington, DC, to pursue a PhD program at Howard University while working at Howard University.

Without hesitation, she passed along my phone number to him. And just like that, fate stepped in. We spoke over the phone and quickly formed a friendship, which blossomed into something truly special—we married. His name was Dr. Basliel W. Gabriel. Basliel was a brilliant cancer research scientist whose work brought hope to many. Tragically, he passed away at the age of 65 in 2012 after battling the very disease he had dedicated his career to understanding. His loss was profound, but his legacy endures in two incredible blessings: our children. Our son was 27 then, and our daughter was 24. Basliel's legacy lives on through his scientific contributions and our family, a living testament to the serendipitous events that brought us together.

With every small step, I inched closer to my dreams, overcoming each obstacle through sheer determination and faith. My passion for learning was unrelenting, and once I set my sights on a goal, nothing could sway me. I worked tirelessly, often sacrificing my social and family life to see my dreams come to fruition. For me, progress, no matter how incremental, was deeply fulfilling. Each achievement, however modest, was a testament to my relentless drive. This journey—one that required grit, resilience, and a willingness to embrace the unknown—felt divinely guided, as if my path was always meant to unfold this way.

Eager to advance my career, I left the position at Bowie State College to join a private insurance firm. This decision opened new doors and allowed me to immerse myself in a world I was only beginning to understand. In the America of the 1970s, few avenues led upward for a Black woman, an immigrant, and a business novice. Yet, I pressed on, juggling multiple responsibilities, including the management of a small chain of lobby shops and learning the language of business with each step. I studied diligently, taking professional courses to hone my skills, even as I prepared to become a mother. There were mornings when I would rise before dawn, preparing my shops for the day, before heading off to work. Looking back, I marvel at the energy, the determination, and, above all, the faith that carried me through those days.

I've had many mentors who placed their faith in me, and they remain in my heart to this day. Among them was my college counselor, Mrs. Atkins, who showed me generosity and kindness. She would invite me to her home and even offered me her car to drive. Believe it or not, the car was a yellow Jaguar sports car. This unbelievable kindness to trust a young person with a sports car was transformative, showing me that America, for all its complexities, is a place where people from diverse backgrounds can support and uplift each other. Some people created an environment of goodwill and compassion as natural human beings. In those days, Americans were more organic, God-fearing, and more gentle. Graduated from Bowie, worked at Bowie, and left Bowie to venture and lead my life in a different arena.

While working for the Great West Life, I opened gift shops in different areas of the Metro DC vicinity without giving up my office job. I remember one incident when I was working in the office. I had a lot of keys on my keychain placed on my desk. These keys were keys for my different gift shops, and one of the staff members in the office observed those keys on my desk and said, "Sam, what do you do with all these keys?" He called me Sam instead of Zed. I guess that is my plantation name. He was too good to remember my real name. Anyhow, instead of saying the keys on my desk are my shop keys, I replied to him, "'J', the keys you see on my desk are office keys, as I work as an office cleaner at night." He seemed happy that I worked as an office cleaner at night. Believe it or not, I have so many real stories like this.

My journey has been shaped by resilience and determination. After working at Bowie State, spending nine years with a private insurance firm, and owning and running some gift shops on the side, I decided to pursue a restaurant business. In 1988, I opened a restaurant in Georgetown, Washington, DC; we called it Zed's Ethiopian Cuisine when Ethiopian cuisine was unfamiliar to most. I saw an opportunity to share my heritage with Washingtonians, using my education and determination to introduce Ethiopian food to a new audience.

Running a restaurant led me down yet another path of learning and growth, but proved more challenging than I could have ever imagined. This venture demanded that I give up a steady office job to pour my heart and soul into my business, a decision that felt both risky and exhilarating. And while I kept this endeavor hidden from my father—fearing it would worry him—my hard work ultimately paid off. Honestly, I did not disappoint my father or my mother. I was a responsible, ambitious, and disciplined young person.

To navigate the competitive restaurant industry, I joined The Restaurant Association of Metro Washington, eventually serving as its chairperson for a year. Later, I joined the National Restaurant Association as a Board Member, representing the local community for over eight years. Those years taught me invaluable lessons about leadership, perseverance, and the intricacies of running a business.

Success, however, didn't come quickly. The first three years were grueling. Building the restaurant took relentless effort—sweat, sleepless nights, and an unshakable resolve. As they say, "Success without hard work exists only in the dictionary." Eventually, my restaurant gained recognition, becoming a beloved establishment in Georgetown. After twenty-three years, I opened a second location in Gainesville, Virginia.

By then, I was tired and yearning for a fresh start. I decided to sell the business, but what followed was a nightmare I never anticipated. An undercover agent approached me, pretending to be an interested buyer. Trusting his intentions, I shared ideas to improve the restaurant's revenue, mentioning that while I chose not to operate after 11:00 PM to balance family life, a new owner could extend hours to boost bar sales. This innocent comment was twisted, and I was falsely accused of operating unofficially after hours to collect extra unrecorded cash.

What followed was a devastating ordeal. The IRS investigation began that same month, and the stress, anxiety, and anger triggered a stroke. I could not believe such injustice could occur in America. The investigation dragged on for five excruciating years, with long periods of inactivity that gave me false hope that the case was closed. The prolonged uncertainty created both a financial and health crisis.

Unfamiliar with the legal system, I naively extended the statute of limitations when requested, trusting that my innocence would prevail. I lacked legal counsel initially, and when I found representation, it was a lengthy and costly process. My previous lawyer had taken a government job and could no longer assist me. As the saying goes, *"Justice delayed is justice denied."* The drawn-out process drained me emotionally, financially, and physically.

Despite everything, I still marvel at how much strength I've gained from this journey. It is an unbelievable story of resilience in the face of an unjust system, but it's also a reminder of how fragile life can be when the systems meant to protect us fall short.

Success, I discovered, was not a solitary journey. It required support, kindness, and a community that believed in me when I faced adversity. I was fortunate to meet people who saw potential in me, like the owner of my restaurant's building. She believed in me enough to offer me a refinancing option to secure the property—a gesture I will forever hold close. That experience led me to own nine properties in later years. Her belief and generosity exemplified the very best of human connection and compassion.

My journey, as with many immigrant stories, was not without challenges. I encountered prejudice and skepticism, often being viewed through the lens of my race, gender, and immigrant background. There were people who could not comprehend my success, attributing it to anything but my own hard work. Some people thought I had another organization or person behind me. But for every person who doubted me, there were countless others who lifted me. America, to me, remains a land of potential, filled with good-hearted individuals who stand for justice and equity. I remain grateful to those who saw my worth and understood that my journey, struggles, and triumphs, are a testament to determination and resilience. I focused on fulfilling my purpose on this earth. I believe everyone has a purpose if we stop to listen and believe in ourselves.

The Thread of Purpose: In a quiet town nestled between rolling hills, there lived an old weaver named Mara. She spent her days at her loom, crafting intricate tapestries that told stories of the town's history, its seasons, and its people. To outsiders, her work seemed simple, even trivial in a world rushing toward modernity. But to Mara, weaving was more than a craft—it was her purpose.

One day, a young man named Theo, disillusioned by the monotony of his life, visited Mara's workshop. "Why do you bother with this?" he asked. "No one really notices your tapestries. What's the point?" Mara smiled and gestured for Theo to sit. She pointed to a nearly completed tapestry on her loom. It depicted a vast tree with deep roots and vibrant leaves, but there was an unfinished patch where the threads hung loose and tangled.

"See this?" she said, holding up a single thread. "Alone, it seems insignificant. But when woven into the tapestry, it becomes part of a story—a story that gives it purpose."

Theo frowned. "But how does that matter? What difference does it make if the story is told or not?"

Mara paused and then replied, "Purpose isn't just about grand outcomes; it's about the act of weaving itself. It's what makes our lives meaningful, even if the world doesn't always notice. Without purpose, we're like these loose threads—scattered, disconnected. With it, we create something larger than ourselves."

Theo thought about this. His own days felt like loose threads, directionless and empty. He realized it wasn't the lack of recognition or success that troubled him—it was the absence of a guiding thread in his life. Over time, Theo began exploring what gave him joy and fulfillment. He found purpose in teaching music to children in the town, seeing how it lit up their faces and gave them confidence. His days, once heavy with monotony, now felt rich with meaning.

Years later, as Mara wove her final tapestry, the townspeople came together to celebrate her work. Each tapestry she'd made hung around the town square, telling a story not just of their town, but of a life well-lived. Mara's threads, seemingly insignificant on their own, had indeed created something beautiful and enduring. Purpose, Mara had shown, isn't about fame or fortune. It's the quiet force that gives our days direction and our lives depth. It's the thread that connects us to ourselves, to others, and to something greater than we can see.

Zed Wondemu with Mike Tyson.

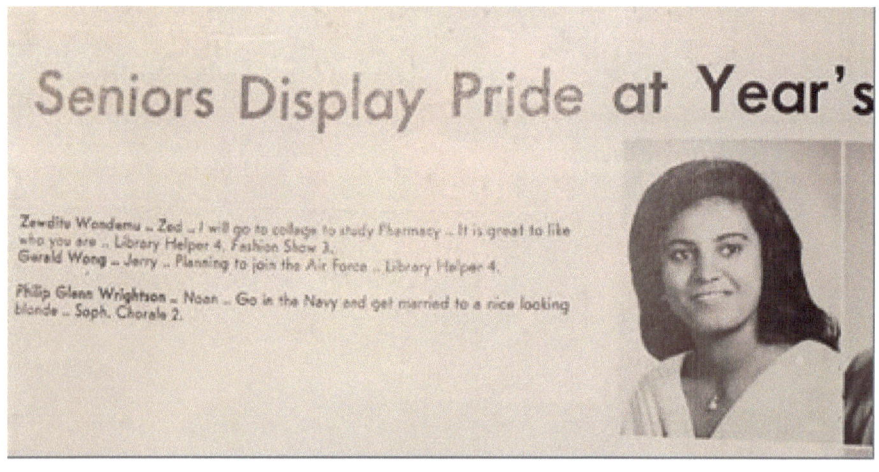

Zed's Senior High School Year Book Picture.

Chapter One

Shattered American Dream

My early years in America were filled with hope and promise. I completed my high school education here, continued to college, and even pursued a master's degree, twice. While running my restaurant, I earned an additional master's degree in business from the University of Maryland University College. I believed wholeheartedly in the American dream and in the values that this country stood for. America, to me, was a land of opportunity, one that rewarded hard work, perseverance, innovation, and creativity.

For years, I was a staunch advocate of the American system, defending its ideals at home and abroad. But after September 11, everything changed. For those of us with foreign names, life became filled with suspicion. I never thought my identity would cast a shadow over my accomplishments, nor that my hard work and devotion to this country could be questioned so easily.

For years, I poured my heart into my business, creating jobs and opportunities for others, always striving to uphold a high level of integrity. Yet, as I began to find success, it seemed that my achievements drew scrutiny. Suddenly, my intelligence, my character, and even my intentions were being questioned. This was not what I expected in a country that celebrated diversity and welcomed hard work. I didn't understand why this was happening, especially after earning my education in America, competing alongside my fellow Americans, and contributing positively to the system.

I thought my dedication to the American dream would earn me respect, but instead, I found myself under relentless scrutiny. As a woman, an immigrant, and a Black entrepreneur, my every success was dissected and, at times, met with thinly veiled skepticism. Despite my contributions, there were moments when I felt treated as a second-class citizen, my ambition was often met with doubt rather than encouragement.

I was proud when I opened my restaurant in the heart of Georgetown, Washington DC. I felt like an ambassador, introducing Ethiopian cuisine and culture to the American public. For me, food was more than just a business—it was a bridge, a way to foster cultural understanding and share the warmth and richness of Ethiopian traditions. I took great pride in representing Ethiopia and showing what could be achieved in America with hard work, resilience, and faith regardless of how some skeptics told me I would lose my shirt soon. I proved them wrong as I stayed in the restaurant business for more than 23 years.

America stands apart as a nation unlike any other. Its uniqueness is woven into its history, culture, and values, making it a land of extraordinary opportunity, diversity, and innovation. From its founding ideals to its global influence, America's character is shaped by a blend of ambition, resilience, and an ever-evolving spirit.

One of the defining features of the United States is its diverse population. Often described as a melting pot or a salad bowl, America has welcomed people from all corners of the world, each bringing their traditions, languages, and perspectives. This fusion of cultures enriches society and also fuels creativity, progress, and collective strength that continues to shape the nation.

At its core, America was built on principles of democracy, liberty, and individual rights. The Constitution and the Bill of Rights ensure fundamental freedoms, including speech, religion, and the press. These rights serve as the foundation of the country's identity, making it a symbol of freedom and self-governance in the eyes of the world.

Beyond its ideals, America's economic strength is unmatched. As one of the largest economies on the planet, it thrives on capitalism and entrepreneurship. From towering financial districts to the garages where billion-dollar companies were born, the country's dedication to innovation is evident. Industries such as technology, entertainment, and aerospace have positioned the United States as a leader in shaping the modern world. Silicon Valley, in particular, has become a beacon of progress, pioneering advancements in artificial intelligence, space exploration, and digital technology.

The land itself is as diverse as its people. From the vast Grand Canyon to the towering peaks of the Rocky Mountains, from the glaciers of Alaska to the volcanoes of Hawaii, America's landscapes are breathtaking and varied. These natural wonders, along with the country's rich resources, have played a significant role in its growth and prosperity.

On the world stage, America wields unparalleled influence. Its military strength ensures national security and plays a crucial role in global stability. As a leader in international diplomacy, the United States helps shape policies, forge alliances, and promote democratic values around the world.

Yet, America's influence is not limited to politics or economics. It is deeply embedded in global culture. From Hollywood's cinematic masterpieces to the music that fills stadiums worldwide, American entertainment has an undeniable reach. The NBA and NFL captivate audiences across continents, while the voices of American artists and storytellers inspire generations.

Science and discovery have long been at the heart of America's journey. From the moon landing to the creation of the internet, the nation has been a driving force behind groundbreaking innovations. NASA continues to push the boundaries of space exploration, while leading universities such as Harvard, MIT, and Stanford remain at the forefront of medical and technological advancements. These institutions draw the brightest minds worldwide, ensuring that America remains a hub of knowledge and progress.

The strength of the nation also lies in its resilience. Throughout history, America has faced economic crises, social upheavals, and global challenges, yet time and again, it has emerged stronger. Civil rights and women's rights movements are testaments to the country's ability to evolve, adapt, and fight for justice.

America has flaws but remains a land of ambition, opportunity, and reinvention. Its extraordinary nature is defined not only by its successes but also by its willingness to confront its struggles and push forward. In a constantly changing world, America continues to shape the future, proving its uniqueness is not just in what it has accomplished, but in the boundless possibilities of what it has yet to achieve.

My love for this country is unshakable, and I will always treasure the years of happiness and success I experienced here. America encouraged me to pursue my dreams and build a life for my family. Yet, the shadow of suspicion and the threat of being misunderstood haunted me. It pains me to think that in the land of opportunity, our intelligence is still questioned simply because of our background or skin color. My experience is based on both gratitude and deep sorrow—a reminder of the complex, sometimes contradictory nature of this beautiful nation. The racist nature of some hinders the success and accomplishments of black citizens as if we are not supposed to pass the demarcation line the system set for us in wealth. The mentality of greedy agencies and individuals made it difficult as if all the good is good for them not for black people. The scale of measurement has a flow. Our intelligence is questioned as if God gave two types of brains to humans.

I was shocked when the prosecutor was defining my lifestyle to the judge to make his points by saying, "Your honor, she lives in a big house, she drives an expensive car, and she contributes money to different charitable entities," as if owning a big house in America is a big deal. I do not understand why he made it a big deal to the extent of mentioning this silly stuff to the judge. I did not understand what he was trying to prove. If one works hard, not only that my husband is a professional cancer researcher but his income and my income of course helped us to progress better. Amazingly, some of us are not expected to have a good life as if a good life only belongs to the selective few or a special group. That is the reason why I say do not question my God-given intelligence. Why are there question marks when we show financial growth?

Chapter Two
Undue Diligence

I've always believed that talent, education, and hard work are the foundations of a fulfilling life. America, my adopted country, allowed me to put these qualities to use and to thrive on my own terms. With every success, I aimed to be transparent, honest, and, above all, fair. Business, to me, was never just about profits—it was about lifting others, providing opportunities, and practicing a kind of compassionate capitalism. I wanted to make a difference and show that hard work, combined with heart, could yield beautiful results.

From the beginning, I was an open book. My staff, friends, and family always knew where I stood. Transparency came naturally to me, not out of pride but because I believed honesty was the simplest and most enduring path. People trusted me, and that trust became one of my most treasured assets. I valued my relationships deeply, and though some saw my straightforwardness as arrogance, I never compromised on my principles.

Throughout my journey, I was blessed with mentors and supporters who believed in me. Dr. Samuel L. Myers at Bowie State University, my late husband, and even my father—all saw potential in me and encouraged me to pursue my dreams without fear. My father's sacrifices to pay for my school, from funding my education to instilling in me a fierce sense of responsibility, set the stage for my success. My late husband's kindness and support allowed me to pursue my ambitions, and together, we shared a life built on respect and understanding.

Despite this support, there were hurdles that tested my resolve. At times, the bad apples in America questioned my intelligence and my ambition. Likely if one is in public life like I was, one encounters a lot of admirers and a few jealous people too. I believe that is part of life. The best thing to do is to be calm and positive. If possible, teach those who are negative by being a positive example because they couldn't reconcile my success with their expectations of what a Black immigrant woman could achieve. There were those who would rather see me as a janitor than a businesswoman, who viewed my hard work with disdain instead of admiration. I learned early that not everyone would celebrate my achievements.

But I refused to be discouraged. I saved diligently from a young age, built my business carefully, and worked toward owning a restaurant and some properties. Each obstacle only strengthened my resolve. My journey was not one of victimhood but of resilience, persistence, and sacrifice. I put everything on the line—time, family, finances—to reach my goals. In the end, my achievements were not mine alone; they were shared with those who had believed in me, those who had shown me kindness, and those who had supported my dreams.

America was a land of opportunity, and I seized that opportunity with gratitude and determination. But over time, I began to see that there were others who could not understand, who could not bear the thought of a Black immigrant woman achieving independence and success. They questioned my abilities, viewed my intelligence with suspicion, and doubted my intentions. And though I knew there were few, their voices were loud enough to sow seeds of doubt.

I am grateful to the countless Americans who welcomed me, encouraged me, and taught me to believe in my potential. These are the people who embody the American spirit—kind, hardworking, and fair. I remain in awe of them. But there is a small minority that cannot accept the success of others, a group that preaches equality but cannot bear to see it in action. I continue to be inspired by the values of compassion and integrity, and I choose to honor the goodness I've encountered over the years. The generosity of spirit I found in America will always be greater than the small-mindedness of a few.

Chapter Three

Hurt, Blindsided, and Humiliated

In the wake of a fresh presidential inauguration, on May 27, 2009—a season meant to represent progress and hope—I found myself wounded and profoundly depleted. The irony of it all sat heavy in my heart. I kept asking myself, "Why?" What could have triggered such an intense and hostile intrusion into my life? Was it because of my involvement with the presidential campaign? My advocacy work and testimony on April 15, 2002, town hall meeting led by Congressman, Dick Armey where I spoke up for fair tax reform? Or was it simply because I dared to open a new restaurant in the throes of a recession, daring to pursue my dreams despite adversity?

I was not just puzzled; I was hurt, blindsided, and humiliated. I was hurt because when I was in college, I was taught to exercise freedom of speech, freedom of opinion and ideas, and freedom of aligning to any political party in America, Republican or Democrat. That is the beauty of the American political system.

That Thursday morning began like any other. I dropped my daughter off at the gym around 7:00 AM, a ritual she maintained before heading to her summer classes at Marymount University. I asked her father to pick her up afterward, and I returned home to get ready for the day to go to the restaurant. It was early and quiet, with only my thoughts keeping me company as I prepared for work. My son was in California visiting a friend, leaving the house unusually calm.

Then the silence shattered.

A relentless banging at the door pulled me from my shower, each knock louder and more demanding than the last. My first thought was that something had happened to my son in California; panic rushed through me as I imagined the worst. Frantically, I threw on what little I had nearby—a nightgown, barely covering me—as I ran to the door, opening it wide in a haze of dread. Before I knew it, several men stormed in, barking orders and demanding I put my hands up. I kept on voicing that you are in the wrong house. I literally thought they came into my house by mistake. It seemed like an address error.

They didn't ask questions. They didn't explain. They took control of my home, searching each room, calling out as though they were in hostile territory, while I stood there, vulnerable and exposed. I could only feel grateful that my children weren't home to witness this scene. After what felt like a lifetime, they identified themselves as part of an IRS investigation, there to search my home, and my restaurant. *I asked why they hadn't simply conducted an audit,* the legal process I thought was in place for these things. The response was hollow and offered no explanation. My heart felt like it was shriveling in my chest; my mouth was dry, and my skin, in those moments, seemed to grow darker with a mixture of anxiety, anger, and despair. I thought I had left a life of oppressive practices behind when I stayed here in America to avoid a military government. But standing there that day, I questioned everything.

I had poured myself into building an honest life and business here. My taxes, both personal and professional, were always prepared by a reputable accounting firm. But when I reached out to my accountant in the hours that followed, seeking his guidance and support, he refused to stand with me. Days later, he even resigned from my case, leaving me abandoned and alone in a fight I barely understood. The fight does not make any sense.

I had always prided myself on the meticulous way I managed my records, down to every label on every box. I had invested in a state-of-the-art POS system for my restaurant—a decision that was both costly and forward-thinking, as most small businesses weren't using such systems back then. But that day, I questioned whether any of it was worth it. My honesty and dedication now felt naive, perhaps even foolish, in a world that seemed to reward deception over integrity; corruption over honesty; impropriety over integrity.

I hired a lawyer, hoping for clarity and justice, but even he was met with vagueness and hostility. His letters demanding an explanation were met with silence. He sent them a letter indicating that their actions were an act of harassment. It became clear that I wasn't simply under scrutiny; I was being harassed and subjected to a kind of psychological assault that went beyond any single act of prejudice. It was modern-day lynching since I was found in the room of success instead of in the room of beggars. It felt like punishment—not for doing wrong, but for succeeding, for stepping beyond the boundaries that some believed were drawn around my race, my gender, and my background.

During this tough time, I received an email from a dear friend which made me so emotional that I decided to open my heart to her.

Hello from here!

carolkline@comcast.net carolkline@comcast.net

To: zed@zeds.net

Zed Wondemu zed@zeds.net

Thu, Nov 12, 2009 at 9:48 PM

Hi, my dear sister,

I have been thinking about you so much since you called. I put you and your family on my nightly prayer list, so whether you want prayers or not, you're getting them!

I've been so bad about my friendships these past few years. I allowed myself to become a workaholic and to convince myself that that was okay because it was for a good cause. Well, it was for a good cause, but no one is more important than friends/family. I miss you. I miss our good talks. I miss your restaurant. I know that in another century, communications will be totally different in this country (and in other countries, too, of course). In 100 years, I will have a big screen in my office so I can see you while we talk. You will have the same. But in 100 years, I'll be 171 years old, so I guess there's no sense in waiting for that.

It's gotten so cold out here-in the 40s. I read that much of Virginia got sloshed with Ida. I hope you are OK. It's good that you don't live on the coast. But all that rain could not be good for business.

Each time we talk, it breaks my heart a little because I know you have things you want to say, but you cannot say them over the telephone. I want to hear what you want to share, but I don't know how to do that unless you want to try by email. I hope you will do that. "Aborted Dream" is a terrible title for a life and I wish I could hug my sister and make things better for you. I know I can't, but I do love you and wish you well. You have such a great heart. You are one of the very best people I know.

Love,
Carol

Carol's words cut deeply, but they brought comfort too. She was right. I had dared to believe in the American dream, to think that hard work and integrity would be enough to shield me from the ugliness that hides in some hearts. But, as her email reminded me, not everyone saw me as I saw myself; to some, I was an anomaly to be contained. So, I wrote my reply to her:

Zed Wondemu zed@zeds.net

To: carolkline@comcast.net, Zed Wondemu zed@zeds.net

Fri, Nov 13, 2009 at 1:04 PM

Dear Carol,

I am glad you keep my family and me in your prayers. Both of us need prayer so badly.

On May 27, 2009, I took my daughter to the gym to do her ritual exercise before going to her summer school. I dropped her before 7:00 am and asked her dad to drop her at Mary Mount University, in Arlington and I went home to shower and work. It was Thursday morning and my son was in California to visit his good friend, Micheal. I took my shower and came out and I was naked and I heard my door banging. First, I thought my daughter and her Dad came back to pick up something. But the door-banging business continued very harshly. By this time, my heart was pounding thinking something had happened to my son and that's why a lot of people were outside banging the door. I ran down the stairs thinking about my son- and I opened the door and asked all those outside to come in. One of the guys told me, "Hands up!" I put my hands up and asked him what I did? Did I kill someone? I was told to sit down – Mind you I did not even have my underwear or proper clothing. I had a clear night cloth on me. These people went to each room shouting "Is anybody home" searching each room.

Finally, I was told they are from the IRS Investigation division and they stated they came to collect all documents and search the house and the restaurant in Georgetown simultaneously. I kept on asking "Why did you audit me?" "Why are you doing this to me?" My mouth was dry and my skin was darker than it is with disappointment and madness. Carol, I am mad. I left Ethiopia and got adopted by this country so that no one will have a right to come to my house or business to harass me. I gave up my country and my own mother for freedom and human rights. Carol-I am in tears even now while I am composing this email. I do not know what happened. A notable accountant prepares all my business taxes, including my taxes. I keep all my records in decent shape. I am always careful about keeping records; in fact it was kept so well in each box labeled with the exact date and year. What a tragedy the whole story is. I am still under investigation; you know I have not done anything. I have a lawyer, but neither of us has not heard anything, and I am not charged with anything. In the process, my reputation and my business are now destroyed. After September 11, everyone with a foreign name is a suspect of a bad deed. This is harassment.

Carol – You do not know – how I am damaged psychologically and emotionally and I do not have any more drive or interest to do my job. I am completely destroyed. So far, I have not heard anything yet to know exactly what I did. I believed in this country and trusted the system so much and I feel like I lost my country (USA). It feels I am betrayed, It feels so many things and I cannot tell you everything.

Carol! I am mad!

ZED

The days after the raid felt like drowning in slow motion. My home, once a place of warmth and safety, now felt tainted and violated. I couldn't walk down the stairs without remembering the

16

way they stormed in, without feeling the ghost of that cold command—hands up. I had lived through hardship, through the struggles of building a life from nothing, but never had I felt so powerless. This was psychological rape.

At night, sleep would not come. Every time I closed my eyes, I was back in that moment, standing half-dressed in my own home, my body exposed not to their eyes but to their judgment. I had done nothing wrong, yet I was treated like a criminal. The walls seemed to close in on me, suffocating me with thoughts that refused to quiet: Why did this happen? Will they come back? Am I still under investigation? The silence from the authorities was unbearable—no charges, no explanations, just destruction and abandonment.

And then there was the anger. A deep, relentless fury that burned inside me, stronger than the fear, stronger than the humiliation. I had given everything to this country. I had built a business, created jobs, and paid my taxes. I had done everything right, and yet, one morning, they had torn it all down without so much as an answer. I had left Ethiopia, my homeland, believing I was coming to a place where I would be free, where no government could take away what I worked for. But that dream felt like a cruel joke now. My name, identity, and my very existence—suddenly, they were enough to make me suspect. I wasn't an entrepreneur, a mother, or a citizen anymore. I was just foreign. And that was enough.

The worst part was how it broke something inside me. I used to wake up with purpose, ready to push forward, to build, and to create. But now? I could barely get out of bed. My restaurant, my passion, felt like a burden. The drive that once carried me through impossible odds was gone. I had always believed in justice, and fairness, in the idea that hard work would be rewarded. But now I know the truth: *justice delayed is justice denied.* And I was just another person waiting, knowing it might never come.

I began to understand the words of my friend, a kind, honest person who happens to be a Caucasian white woman, who upon hearing my story, reached out to offer words of compassion and outrage. In her response email, she wrote:

"You did nothing to bring that disaster down on your beautiful head. You just didn't understand the depth of the racism in rural Virginia. You were too successful, too confident, too happy, too well-dressed—none of that fit the image those people wanted to see in a Black woman. But you didn't know all that because you were Ethiopian. You made wonderful things happen in your life because you believed you could. The problem wasn't yours. It was theirs."

As I read Carol's words, my hands trembled. I felt the breath hitch in my throat, my vision blurring as the weight of her truth settled deep into my bones. You did nothing to bring that disaster down on your beautiful head. The sentence rang in my mind, over and over, as if I needed to convince myself that it was true. For months, I had been drowning in self-doubt, wondering if I had made a mistake, if I had missed something, if I had unknowingly invited this nightmare into my life. But Carol, with her unwavering clarity, stripped those doubts away in a single breath.

I wasn't the problem. They were.

I let out a sob I hadn't realized I was holding.

All this time, I had been blaming myself—thinking maybe I hadn't done enough, hadn't been careful enough, hadn't played the game the right way. But I had done everything right. I worked hard, I played by the rules, I built something beautiful out of nothing. And still, they came for me.

Carol put into words something I had been too afraid to acknowledge. I had been blind to the full force of what it meant to be Black in America. Not just Ethiopian. Not just an immigrant. But

18

a Black woman who had dared to succeed, to be confident, to believe in her own worth. I had come to this country with a belief in justice, in fairness, in the idea that hard work would always be enough. I had been so proud of what I had built, of the life I had carved out for my children. But to them—the nameless, faceless system that had crushed me—I was never supposed to have it.

Tears spilled down my cheeks, my body shaking with the force of emotions I had tried so hard to suppress. Anger. Pain. Grief. A deep, soul-crushing grief—not just for my business, my reputation, or even my sense of security, but for the illusion I had lost. The illusion that I was safe, that I was free, that I belonged.

Carol saw me in a way I hadn't even seen myself. She named the thing I had been too wounded to name. I wasn't a failure. I wasn't a criminal. I wasn't even a mistake. I was simply too much for them— too successful, too happy, too sure of myself in a way they couldn't accept.

I pressed my hands to my face, trying to hold in the flood of emotions, but it was impossible. I wept, for myself. For years I had believed in a dream that had betrayed me. For the pain of knowing that no matter how much I gave, it might never be enough.

But beneath the sorrow, something else stirred. A slow, burning ember.

If they wanted me to disappear, to crumble under the weight of their injustice, they would be disappointed. Because now, I understand. Now, I saw the truth.

And I would not be silent.

In Ethiopia, we have a dish called Shiro, made from ground peas and spices, cooked slowly until it thickens and bubbles. When left uncovered, it can splatter and make a mess. But with a lid, it's contained, simmering quietly. Perhaps my life, my success, had become like that of Shiro—something they felt needed to be covered, contained, and kept in its place. What they do not realize is my talent, my intelligence, and work habits are given to me by God, my creator with some purposeful destiny that *no one can stop or seal.*

I am not blind to the fact that tax matters require scrutiny; I do not deny nor undermine the need for accountability. But there is a way to ask questions without tearing a person's dignity apart, without assuming that every success in a person like me must come from something unearned or undeserved. There is a way to uphold justice without erasing someone's humanity in the process. Especially the justice I expect from America.

The strange part was after checking me with a microscope for *five years of investigation*, they had to revise the expenses I claimed on my tax returns without consulting an accountant from my side and came up with *$50,000 in four years*. They fabricated the story assuming they had to come up with something to justify the five years of investigation, harassment, and discomfort to me and to my family. A tax issue with fabricated discrepancy took five years to investigate. Brilliant!

It has been a long and painful journey. But with each challenge, I have learned. I have grown stronger. I have come to understand that endurance, resilience, and the fierce love I hold for my family, my work, and myself will always be more powerful than the forces that seek to diminish and destroy me for unknown reasons of cruelty.

This was how the saga began. And though it left scars, it did not break me. Instead, it pushed me like a propeller to excel more, to create a strong relationship with my Creator. "If God is for me, who could be against me?" They did not know they were fighting with a person with a strong spiritual identity. In the process, I learned vengeance is His not mine. Somehow they will pay for this, the divine power will intervene and a payback time will come.

Five Years for a Fabricated $50,000

When the IRS arrives with raid jackets and badges, it doesn't feel like "due diligence."

It feels like a warning: We have the power to ruin you.

That's how it began for me.

An early-morning knock. Agents on my porch. Boxes of files were carried out of my house. Computers seized. Neighbors watching. No charges, just a vague explanation that my taxes "warranted closer examination."

That "closer examination" became my life for the next five years.

Every check, every deposit, every invoice, pulled apart and inspected.

My business slowed to a crawl. Clients left, fearing their names might be dragged into the storm. My savings bled away into legal bills. My family lived under a cloud of suspicion.

And for what?

At the end of this marathon investigation, thousands of man-hours, mountains of paperwork, the IRS announced its "finding": a supposed $50,000 misstatement.

I knew it was wrong. The number didn't even exist in his records. It was a fabrication, an invention stitched together from half-true assumptions and willful misinterpretation.

But by then, I was exhausted.

Fighting it meant more years in the grinder. More bills. More headlines.

So, I settled, not because I was guilty, but because it was cheaper to pay for a lie than to keep paying for my freedom.

This is undue diligence in its most dangerous form: not a search for truth, but a demonstration of force. Five years of disruption, intimidation, and economic wreckage, just to conjure a number significant enough to justify the raid that started it all.

In the end, the IRS didn't just "find" $50,000. They manufactured it, then used it as proof that their five-year campaign was somehow warranted.

That's not tax enforcement.

That's a warning to every citizen: We can knock on your door, tear apart your life, and if we can't find something… we can make something.

This is a true example of undue diligence…

Zed with her children and daughter-in-law in Korean attire.

Zed Wondemu with her children.

Chapter Four

My Journey in the Restaurant Business

In 1988, I opened Zed's Ethiopian Restaurant, at a time when Ethiopian cuisine was not as widely recognized and available as it is today. My journey into the restaurant industry was not conventional, nor was it something I had initially planned. However, as with many life-changing ventures, it was born from an unexpected opportunity and a deep sense of purpose.

A Fortunate Friendship and an Unexpected Opportunity

The idea of opening a restaurant was inspired by a dear friend who cared for me after the birth of my second child. Following my C-section, she prepared delicious Ethiopian meals for me, offering nourishment and companionship. Her kindness lifted my spirits, sometimes making me laugh so hard that it strained my stitches.

One day, she proposed that we open an Injera bakery together. She had prior experience launching an Injera bakery and was the first person to introduce Injera made from real Teff flour. Before her, most people used regular wheat flour to make Injera. She approached me as a potential business partner because of my experience owning and operating gift shops. However, I was not particularly interested in running a bakery. Not one to give up easily, she suggested another idea—an Ethiopian restaurant. This idea resonated with me, as it was a business that aligned more with my interests. More importantly, I wanted to support my friend's dream and help her showcase her incredible cooking skills.

We embarked on this journey together, her culinary talent complemented by my financial investment and business experience.

However, after just one year, she found the restaurant business too demanding and chose to step away. Though we parted ways, we did so amicably and with mutual respect. Her departure left me to navigate an unfamiliar industry alone, but I was determined to move forward; for some reason, I enjoyed challenges.

Facing the Challenges of the Restaurant Industry

I had no background in running a restaurant. My experience was in academia, I had attended college and graduate school, worked for a college president, and later transitioned into the private sector, working for an insurance company while managing my gift shops. Despite lack of food industry experience, I believed embracing challenges was essential for personal and professional growth.

The first two years were particularly tough. Business was slow, and I had to rethink my approach. Realizing that I needed to promote the restaurant actively, I took a proactive stance. I contacted nearby universities like Georgetown and George Washington, directly engaging with students and faculty to introduce them to Ethiopian cuisine. This strategy proved effective as students began dining at the restaurant, and professors started hosting meetings with their students there. Additionally, Ethiopian taxi drivers played a crucial role in supporting my business, often gathering in groups for lunch.

The Power of Marketing and Community Engagement

Recognizing the importance of visibility, I invested heavily in marketing and promotions. I was young, ambitious, and eager to make my restaurant a success. I actively engaged with local business associations, became a member of the Chamber of Commerce, and attended community events to spread awareness of my restaurant.

Instead of focusing solely on Ethiopian customers who were already familiar with the cuisine, I targeted non-Ethiopian patrons, including tourists visiting Washington, D.C. This strategy set Zed's Ethiopian Restaurant apart, as it became a cultural hub where people could not only enjoy Ethiopian food but also learn about Ethiopian traditions and heritage.

At that time, Ethiopian restaurants in Washington, D.C., were still few and far between. Emma Desta opened the first Ethiopian restaurant on Georgia Avenue while I was still in college. She paved the way, and I respect her contribution immensely. When I opened Zed's, it was one of the few Ethiopian restaurants in the city.

Promoting Ethiopian Cuisine on a Larger Scale

Zed's Ethiopian Restaurant became more than just a dining establishment—it became a platform for cultural exchange. As an education major, I saw an opportunity to use my restaurant to teach people about Ethiopian traditions, history, and customs. I accepted invitations from various associations and community organizations to promote Ethiopian food, even when it required significant personal investment without immediate financial returns.

One of my proudest achievements was representing Ethiopian cuisine at major events. Zed's Ethiopian Restaurant was the only Ethiopian establishment among the 40 top restaurants selected to participate in the annual Taste of DC festival on Pennsylvania Avenue. We participated in this event for four consecutive years, helping to popularize Ethiopian food beyond our immediate community. This effort inspired many others to open Ethiopian restaurants in Washington, Maryland, and Virginia. I am glad Zed's Ethiopian Restaurant became an instrument for others to venture freely.

Additionally, we had the honor of serving Ethiopian cuisine in Congress when the Ethiopian Embassy requested that we cater for 40 members of Congress meeting with the Prime Minister of Ethiopia. Zed's was also one of the select few restaurants chosen to participate in President Bill Clinton's first and second inaugurations, further solidifying our reputation in the city.

Ethiopian cuisine is unique in its rich flavors, communal dining experience, and deep cultural significance. The combination of spices, herbs, and slow-cooked stews offers a distinct culinary experience that captures the essence of Ethiopia's diverse regions. Injera, the traditional fermented flatbread, serves as both a staple food and an eating utensil, embodying the values of sharing and togetherness that define Ethiopian dining traditions. Introducing these customs to a wider audience not only enriched their understanding of Ethiopian culture but also helped bridge cultural gaps through food.

As Ethiopian cuisine gained popularity, more people became curious about the health benefits associated with traditional Ethiopian ingredients. Teff, the primary grain used in making injera, is naturally gluten-free and packed with essential nutrients, making it a sought-after superfood in modern health-conscious communities. Many customers who initially came for the experience of trying something new became repeat visitors, drawn not just by the flavors but also by the wholesome, nutritious qualities of Ethiopian dishes. Through these engagements, Zed's Ethiopian Restaurant played a crucial role in fostering a lasting appreciation for Ethiopian food and its cultural heritage.

A Hub for Culture, Politics, and Community Service

Over the years, Zed's Ethiopian Restaurant has become a gathering place for high-ranking officials, celebrities, and tourists alike. It is not just a restaurant but a community space that plays an active role in supporting local initiatives. We contribute to churches, community, and charitable organizations like DC Central Kitchen through financial donations or by offering hands-on training.

One of the initiatives I am most proud of was bringing students from disadvantaged neighborhoods to dine at the restaurant free of charge. Exposing young people to a tablecloth dining experience was deeply rewarding and, in many ways, more meaningful than serving high-profile guests.

Expanding the Ethiopian Culinary Legacy

Ethiopian food has come a long way since I first opened Zed's. Today, Ethiopian restaurants are more common, and the cuisine is celebrated for its unique flavors, communal dining experience, and health benefits. I take great pride in knowing that I played a role in this movement, helping introduce Ethiopian cuisine to a broader audience.

While the restaurant industry is unpredictable and demanding, I would not trade this journey for anything. The experience has taught me resilience, adaptability, and the power of perseverance. It has given me the opportunity to educate others, share my culture, and build a lasting legacy in the heart of Washington, D.C.

A Legacy of Dedication and Gratitude

Over the years, Zed's Ethiopian Restaurant has received numerous accolades, media coverage, and positive reviews from major publications. However, the true measure of success lies in our impact—bringing Ethiopian food into the mainstream, fostering cultural appreciation, and creating a welcoming space for all.

Looking back, I salute the past and present supporters who encouraged and stood by us. Their unwavering support made Zed's Ethiopian Restaurant more than just a business—it became a cornerstone of the community and a celebration of Ethiopian culture.

This journey has been one of resilience, learning, and growth, and I am grateful for every step.

The Inevitable Arrival of Payback Time

Life has a way of balancing the scales, often in ways we least expect. Every action, decision, and effort we put forth carries within it the seed of future consequences. This is the essence of payback time, the moment when the universe, circumstances, or the people around us return the energy we have invested, for better or worse. It is not always immediate, nor always visible, but its arrival is as certain as the turning of the seasons.

Payback time comes because nothing exists in isolation. Acts of kindness, diligence, and integrity build unseen reserves of goodwill and reputation, forming a foundation upon which future rewards are built. Conversely, shortcuts, dishonesty, or neglect of responsibility accumulate like debts on a hidden ledger, waiting for the day they must be reconciled. Life does not forget; it merely bides its time. The seeds planted today, whether in effort or negligence, will inevitably bloom or wither in their due season.

The impact of payback time lies not just in the consequences themselves, but in the lessons it imparts. When success arrives after relentless effort, it is more than a reward, it is validation, proof that perseverance shapes reality. When setbacks occur, they are not mere punishment, but mirrors reflecting the choices made and the paths taken. The timing may feel mysterious, but the principle is clear:

31

energy invested in the world rarely vanishes; it transforms, returning in ways commensurate with the intention behind it.

Understanding that payback time will come can transform the way we approach life. It encourages patience, discipline, and moral clarity. It reminds us that even when immediate results seem elusive, the actions we take today are sowing the future we will one day inherit. This awareness is powerful because it shifts the focus from fleeting gratification to enduring impact, from temporary gain to lasting legacy.

Ultimately, payback time is inevitable. It is the natural rhythm of cause and effect, the echo of our choices reverberating through time. By acting with integrity, diligence, and awareness, we ensure that when the moment of reckoning arrives, it brings fulfillment, opportunity, and justice. And when we experience the return of our efforts, we are reminded that life, in its quiet wisdom, always comes full circle.

Zed with her children and daughter-in-law who she calls her child as well.

Chapter Five

As Far As My Dream

I once heard a preacher, Jentzen Franklin, speak about dreams. His words stirred something within me, as if he had unlocked a code, I'd been searching for all my life. He spoke of dreams as a force that defines us, which unleashes our potential, inspires us, and guides our attitude. A true dream is like a quiet fire, fueling purpose and demanding integrity and discipline. As I listened, I thought about the dreams that had carried me through so many trials, and I felt more determined than ever to keep striving.

For me, dreams were more than aspirations—they were a testament to resilience. Dreams require faith, both in a higher power and in oneself, and they come with a plan: to pray, to plan, to act, and to navigate through the inevitable challenges. Along the way, we meet difficulties that feel like they were placed there to test our resolve. These trials serve as reminders that growth requires sacrifice. Each obstacle, every setback, is a lesson that refines and strengthens us, making our dreams not only achievable but transformative. As the Ethiopian saying indicates Gold gets tested in fire and yet individuals are tested with difficult incidents.' One person's dream does not get fulfilled easily.

I am reminded of those who pursued their dreams later in life. *Ray Kroc built McDonald's at age 54; Colonel Sanders founded KFC at 65. Moses led his people at the age of 80. I think of my own mother, who, at 80, dreamt of building a home for my younger brother. She passed away at 83 before her dream was complete but she showed me that age and circumstances are no match for a soul that dares to dream.*

In my own life, there have been those who believed in my dreams, encouraging me at every step. And then there were those who tried to discredit and undermine me, questioning my talent, my intelligence, and my very right to dream. As a Black woman and an immigrant, I found that my success was often met with suspicion, as though it couldn't possibly be my own achievement. Yet I know that my abilities are gifts from God, my dreams, and His blessings, and no amount of doubt or resentment can take that away from me.

This world, for all its beauty, has its share of people driven by ***envy and malice***. There are those who act not from a place of kindness but from a desire to see others fail. They plant seeds of distrust and division, turning communities and even nations against each other. In my homeland of Ethiopia, I have witnessed leaders exploit tribal loyalties and fuel division for their gain, all while people suffer. The destructive power of hatred, unchecked ambition, and greed is universal, crossing all borders.

But I refuse to let others define my journey. As long as I have dreams, as long as I am willing to act on them, and as long as I am led by faith, I will continue to build and contribute. I believe that each of us has a role to play in creating a world where dreams are encouraged, where hard work is celebrated, and where our shared humanity is honored. In the end, it is not those who doubt us who shape our path but those who inspire us and stand beside us as we pursue our dreams.

My taxes were prepared by a reputable tax accountant and filed on time each year according to the tax law. What bothers me is if the problem was with taxes, why did they investigate me for 5 years and waste the taxpayer's money instead of auditing? As you all know, auditing also comes with pain and struggle. In my case, they should have audited first unless their original investigation intention and aim was something else. A person with the right mind should doubt.

It seems they investigated for five years without any result to their satisfaction, they decided to check my taxes under a microscope to find nothing until they went back to check my expenses and adjusted the expenses according to their wishes without including the tax experts from my side and came up with *$50,000 give and take for 4 years of tax returns. Mind you, for four years.*

The judge, who had a keen sense for reading between the lines, consistently asked if I was being coerced into accepting the plea bargain. She repeated the question multiple times, but I hesitated to admit the truth: I had indeed been pressured, threatened, and forced to accept the plea offer. I feared that if I changed my mind before the judge, they would punish me more severely. I had been warned not to reconsider, to proceed with the plea bargain without resistance. Unaware of legal procedures and possible consequences, I accepted the deal in court, keeping silent about the coercion. I wish I was bold enough to open my mouth to tell her. Yes, I was pinned, pressured, and coerced to accept the plea bargain.

The judge's fairness and diligence gave me a glimmer of faith in the legal system, proving that not everyone in it was indifferent or ruthless. The problem lay with the rookie prosecutor, who was clearly more focused on making a name for himself than on pursuing justice. He targeted me as an easy case to bolster his own reputation, displaying a blatant disregard for fairness. His sole concern was to win the case, not to ensure justice or hear my side. He was rude and power-hungry, and it was clear that the authority he wielded was misused.

That ordeal remains the nastiest experience of my life. The prosecutor was arrogant, ruthless, and fixated on his own success. His disregard for due process and his willingness to damage my life for personal gain will haunt him, I'm sure. Rushing through the case, he didn't hesitate to exploit the system.

The judge's ruling, however, brought a measure of satisfaction. She ordered me to pay the $50,000 settlement at a rate of $100 per month, without interest. Her decision put them in their place. She remarked that, while $50,000 was no small sum, it was unjust to waste five years of taxpayer's money on an unnecessary investigation. She even advised the government prosecutor and his team to convey to his department head that the entire process was flawed. Though I hadn't "won" in the traditional sense, her words gave me a sense of victory. I left the courtroom with renewed respect for her as a judge, grateful for her courtesy, compassion, and the dignity she extended to me. She even wished me luck as I left.

The prosecutor, however, was far from pleased. He pushed for the DC government to pursue additional penalties on the same alleged tax debt, based on calculations he'd made without involving my accountant. Even my lawyer failed to advocate properly on my behalf, often siding with the prosecution. To this day, I can't forget how my attorney seemed complicit in their schemes.

My deepest respect goes to the judge who demonstrated fairness and integrity, seeing through the harassment and understanding the baseless accusations leveled by the prosecutor.

This harrowing experience taught me valuable lessons. Despite its challenges, it underscored the importance of legal education for ordinary citizens. I highly recommend that everyone especially decent, law-abiding people take courses in the U.S. legal system. A foundation in legal knowledge can empower people to protect themselves, even when dealing with their own attorneys.

Zed Wondemu pictured with Hillary Clinton.

38

Chapter Six

Lies

The legal system I once believed in seemed designed to deliver truth and justice. It was a belief deeply rooted in my gratitude for the opportunities this country had given me. But when I found myself under scrutiny, that belief began to fray. My own attorney, the person I'd trusted to defend me, quickly revealed his own self-interest and a surprising willingness to settle rather than seek truth.

Throughout the ordeal, he repeatedly insisted that justice wasn't possible for people like me—that as a minority, I'd never receive fair treatment in the system. But it was his own actions that fed this cycle of injustice. He went along with the prosecutor's claims without questioning their validity, without demanding proof. When he should have been advocating for me, he was urging me to accept the plea bargain. The mere mention of challenging their assertions seemed to unsettle him. Instead, he placed the weight of fear on my shoulders, using it as leverage to force a decision I should never have had to make.

I watched, dismayed, as he raised his voice, dismissed my concerns, and pressured me to accept the bargain, telling me it was my only chance to avoid harsher consequences. He didn't test the evidence, never suggested we call in experts, and never demanded transparency from the prosecution. Instead, he relied on scare tactics, echoing the prosecutor's claims, and each conversation left me feeling more isolated and powerless. The person I had trusted to represent my interests became another instrument in a system bent on breaking my spirit. When I see these types of people who claim they are educated and yet perform savage acts, sometimes I wonder about the purpose of education. I thought education was supposed to make one more humane than barbarian.

The pressure was relentless. I was forced into a choice: accept a deal that contradicted everything I knew about my own innocence or risk facing exaggerated consequences for the very success I had built through hard work. It was a tragic irony. As a citizen who believed in the justice system, I was now painfully aware of its imperfections. The experience felt like the loss of something sacred—as though I were grieving the death of a cherished family member.

And yet, even in this darkness, I found strength. My faith in God and my unwavering sense of self became my only refuge. I realized that while people may try to tarnish what you've built, they cannot erase your truth. People may doubt you, question your character, and threaten your peace, but only God has the power to shape your ultimate destiny. With each attempt to undermine me, I felt a deeper connection to the divine. I knew that no earthly force, no matter how unjust, could take away the integrity I had lived by.

Still, the experience raised painful questions. Why was I, a person who had only sought to contribute, being targeted? Why were lies and distortions so easily accepted over facts and integrity? It broke my heart to realize that while America's justice system claims to uphold truth, it sometimes fails to deliver it. The strange part is if I had not faced this reality and experience, I would not have believed it if anyone had come to me to tell me this kind of experience exists in America. I believe it now, it happened to me.

My journey through this ordeal became a painful reminder that justice is not guaranteed. It's a gift, one that should be guarded fiercely. There are those who use power recklessly, hiding behind laws while betraying their purpose. But as my faith teaches me, truth will prevail, even if the path to it is long and challenging. I chose to believe that no matter what I endured, in the end, justice and truth would find their way back to me. And I hold on to that belief still. Those who were part of the story as a negative force will pay for it directly or indirectly. No one will hide from this unjust act permanently. The law of karma will start haunting them during their lifetime. They will be miserable and unhappy; sick and soulless. I just have to wait, time will tell.

Zed Wondemu pictured with actor John Malkovich.

Chapter Seven

America the Beautiful

In my heart, America has always been a land founded on faith—a country that drew its strength from a belief in God and in principles that transcended politics and power. But somewhere along the way, we seem to have lost that sacred connection. The very mention of God, once woven into the fabric of American society, now feels distant, almost foreign in public life. A nation once proud to honor God now seems hesitant to speak His name.

This shift troubles me deeply. Faith was the compass that guided America's earliest visionaries, that inspired the idea of freedom, and that allowed communities to thrive with shared values. But today, that compass seems misaligned. Where once we sought justice and kindness, we now see a rise in greed and division. The desire for power has overshadowed our moral compass, leaving society vulnerable to forces that exploit rather than uplift.

Growing up, I was taught to view America as a beacon, not just of freedom, but of decency and fairness. This nation promised opportunities to those who were willing to work hard and contribute positively. Its values inspired other countries, setting a standard that people across the globe aspired to follow. America had become a symbol of hope, a testament to what a country could achieve by honoring principles of faith and justice.

But when did we begin to replace these ideals? When did we start prioritizing comfort over conscience, and wealth over wisdom? As I watch America wrestle with issues that divide rather than unite, I feel a deep ache. I long for America that wasn't afraid to believe in something greater, to openly celebrate the virtues of kindness, charity, and faith.

In my home, the mention of God has always been politically correct. And in my life, honoring God has been a foundation that no political shift could alter. For me, God represents hope, resilience, and the possibility of redemption—even in a world shadowed by uncertainty. I see that same potential in America, a potential that can be rekindled by returning to the values that built this nation.

When I think of America the Beautiful, I think of a country that celebrates both individuality and community, that embraces freedom of speech and freedom of faith. I hope that we remember our roots and renew our commitment to justice, fairness, and compassion. Because in a world where people are tempted by power and wealth, the true beauty of America lies in its spirit—a spirit grounded in courage, kindness, and the unwavering pursuit of truth.

45

Chapter Eight
Agent of Chaos

There was a time when I would have placed unwavering trust in the American justice system. I believed it was designed to protect, uphold truth, and serve those who contributed honestly and tirelessly to their communities. But my experience opened my eyes to a different reality, one where justice can sometimes be overshadowed by ambition, prejudice, and misguided power.

I found myself standing against accusations I knew to be false, and I felt the weight of a system more interested in a quick victory than in uncovering the truth. My defense lawyer, rather than challenging the baseless claims, seemed more intent on persuading me to concede, to accept guilt where there was none. He pushed me toward a plea bargain, a "way out" that would spare him the difficulty of defending a case he was either unwilling or unable to fully understand. In addition, unfortunately, he was not a tax lawyer.

In addition, this lawyer did not have any clue about tax and the tax system nor did he seek advice from experts. I can say he did not care, he was bought or threatened by someone. This was not the case in the old days of America. In the old days, if a lawyer detected injustice he would fight to the teeth. Now, everyone chases their interest or lucrative money. Time is changing and their morals change together.

It felt as though I had stepped into a world where success and independence were threats rather than triumphs. Working hard, creating jobs, and pursuing my dreams—these were not crimes, yet they seemed to attract suspicion and doubt. The very qualities I had admired in America—productivity, self-sufficiency, and entrepreneurial spirit—were now being used against me, as though my achievements were somehow evidence of wrongdoing. They make it look like my success is a crime. It is unfortunate not to recognize toil, and work is a good thing, not a bad thing. What kind of lesson are we teaching our children?

I could not understand why those in power had set their sights on me, a hardworking businesswoman when the real threats to this nation went unchallenged. It was a painful realization that some individuals and agencies prioritize self-interest over the collective good, even at the cost of innocent lives and reputations. They appear to thrive on chaos, to sow discord where there could be unity, and to tear down the very foundations that make America strong.

This experience was a harsh reminder that when power is placed in the wrong hands, it becomes a weapon of destruction rather than a tool for justice. There are those who seek to serve, who respect their responsibility and approach it with humility and fairness. But there are others who allow the allure of control to corrupt their intentions, turning them into agents of chaos rather than guardians of peace.

In the end, my ordeal was more than a personal tragedy; it was an awakening to the flaws that can exist within even the most respected institutions. Yet, despite this experience, I hold on to my faith in the principles that first inspired me. I still believe that America can be a land of opportunity and integrity—a place where good people stand up for what is right and refuse to let corruption and ugly acts take root.

This journey has been a test of my resilience, but it has not broken my spirit. I choose to focus on the good, on the countless Americans who embody the kindness, strength, and honesty that drew me to this country. For every agent of chaos, there are many more who serve with honor. And it is in those people that I continue to place my faith.

For every agent of chaos, there are many more who serve with honor. And it is in those people that I continue to place my faith.

In every era, the human story has been shaped by a tension between those who tear down and those who build up. The "agent of chaos" is not always a villain in the traditional sense, sometimes they are a single malicious voice, a manipulator in the shadows, or even a movement fueled by fear and selfish ambition. Their power often lies not in their numbers, but in their willingness to act without restraint, to exploit uncertainty, and to spread distrust like wildfire. Chaos thrives on the spectacle; it captures headlines, monopolizes attention, and leaves many believing that disorder is the dominant force in the world.

But the truth is far more hopeful. For every one person who seeks to destabilize, there are countless others, often unseen, who serve with honor. They are the quiet stewards of stability: the teacher who invests extra time in a struggling student, the medic who treats the wounded without asking which side they are on, the community volunteer who shows up after the cameras leave. They work in the shadows of chaos, repairing the fractures it leaves behind, rarely seeking credit for their resilience.

Honor is not simply about following rules, it is about upholding principles even when no one is watching. Those who serve with honor understand that their actions contribute to something greater than themselves. They may never make headlines, but they safeguard the integrity of communities, institutions, and even humanity itself. In this way, they form a silent majority, a network of guardians holding the line against the erosion of trust and compassion.

My faith lies in these people not because they are flawless, but because they choose, again and again, to act with integrity in an imperfect world. Their presence is a reminder that chaos, no matter how loud, is temporary, while honor, though quiet, is enduring.

Where chaos seeks to divide, honor builds bridges. Where chaos exploits fear, honor plants seeds of understanding. And where chaos leaves scars, honor offers healing.

History teaches us that civilizations survive not by eradicating chaos entirely, that is impossible, but by empowering those who serve with honor to stand together. It is in these people, often unsung and unnoticed, that the true backbone of society resides. When I look toward the future, I do not measure hope by the absence of threats, but by the presence of those willing to face them with courage and conscience.

For every agent of chaos, there are indeed many more who serve with honor. And though chaos may win the moment, honor is what wins the years.

Steadfast Souls and the Quiet Sentinels of Decency

It is in those steadfast souls, those quiet sentinels of decency, that I continue to place my faith, as well as my faith in God. In an age marked by noise, spectacle, and the temptation of expedience, such individuals often go unnoticed. They are not the ones who dominate headlines or seek the glow of public recognition. Instead, they carry out their work in the shadows of ordinary life, upholding the small and often unseen virtues that sustain the moral fabric of society.

These are the men and women who live their values quietly but consistently. They honor their commitments, tell the truth when it is costly, and extend compassion when it is inconvenient. They refuse to bend to cynicism or surrender to despair, not because they are naïve, but because they have anchored themselves to principles that transcend circumstance. In their presence, one senses not merely kindness, but a quiet courage, a moral backbone that does not crack under the strain of difficulty.

Such steadfastness is not born overnight. It is cultivated in the silent crucible of daily choices: a promise kept, a wrong forgiven, a duty fulfilled when no one is watching. In this way, they stand as sentinels, not warriors seeking battle, but guardians maintaining the walls of human decency against the slow erosion of selfishness and moral compromise.

My faith in God strengthens my faith in them, for I see His reflection in their actions. And my faith in them reinforces my faith in God, for they embody what Scripture calls us to be: faithful in the little things, unyielding in the face of temptation, gentle in the presence of weakness. I believe God works not only through grand miracles, but through these living testaments of integrity, whose lives are miracles of quiet endurance.

In times of uncertainty, when corruption, deceit, and cruelty seem to have the louder voice, I recall these sentinels. I picture the teacher who refuses to give up on a struggling student, the caregiver who treats each patient with dignity, the neighbor who offers help without asking for repayment. Their decency is not fragile; it is as enduring as stone, worn smooth by the passing of years yet unbroken.

If civilization is to endure, it will not be saved by slogans or sudden revolutions alone, but by these watchful souls, holding their posts without fanfare. The world may overlook them, but I cannot. For in their faithfulness, I find my hope renewed. And in their quiet strength, I hear an echo of God's enduring love, steady, constant, and accurate.

51

Chapter Nine
Plea-Bargain

After being accused based on false fabricated stories and raided, I hired a lawyer named G. For a long time, we received no explanation for the raid, which eventually forced me to stop using Mr. G's services due to expense. It seemed they stopped; therefore, I did not want to pay the lawyer without work. I then transferred my case to another lawyer, RA. He began discussions with the IRS agent, JL, and eventually met with a group whose identities remain unknown to me, though they were not from the IRS. During this meeting, they presented some figures in their report, and when RA inquired about how the IRS arrived at those numbers, they were unable to explain.

The case lay dormant until November 18, 2014, just before Thanksgiving, when JL and the IRS agent, accompanied by another individual, arrived at my home to deliver a letter instructing me to contact PS from the Justice Department. I was also told to bring my lawyer. However, RA no longer practices law, having taken a position with the DC government, creating a conflict of interest that prevented him from representing me.

In my attempt to find another lawyer, I faced challenges due to the approaching statute of limitations. I later realized they had only five years to finalize their work before the time ran out. Aware of this deadline, while I was not, they pressured me to secure legal representation quickly, threatening to assign me a lawyer if I failed to do so. Ultimately, I was assigned a public defender named TM. They were rushing me; they did not want to wait until I found another lawyer because of the fact the expiration of the statute of limitations was ticking. While searching for a lawyer and comparing fees and negotiating, they decided to assign me a public defendant lawyer, and I did not have any clue that the prosecutor and the lawyer were from the same system.

TM employed tactics that felt like harassment—he cornered me, shouted at me, and pressured me into making swift decisions. His psychological manipulation was overwhelming, leading me to reluctantly accept a plea bargain. Throughout this ordeal, not one of my high-profile contacts offered support, except for my close friends. I learned the hard way that loyalty often comes with strings attached; they were there when I helped them but vanished when I needed assistance.

Despite the absence of support from influential acquaintances, I found strength in my faith. I called upon God daily, seeking justice for the wrongs I faced. I firmly believe that one day, those who wronged me will answer for their actions, both individually and collectively.

The cruelty of my situation was evident in PS's report to the judge, which suggested that I was treated as if I were a hostile nation or organization. I find it incomprehensible that such unjust, arrogant behavior exists in America. If such actions occurred in a third-world country, it might be expected, but witnessing this in the United States is a perplexing reality.

The case of Michael Brown, the eighteen-year-old shot by Officer Wilson in Ferguson, Missouri, further underscores the disparities in our justice system. It astonishes me how Officer Wilson faced no serious questioning, just as I was left without a robust challenge to the so-called evidence presented against me. TM accepted what the prosecutor displayed as if it were gospel truth, and this was a tragic situation.

In the face of this injustice, my only refuge has been my faith. While they may attack me, they will never diminish my belief in

God or my spirit. It is shameful to feel betrayed by a justice system I once trusted.

It is Shameful to Feel Betrayed by a Justice System I Once Trusted to Protect Me

There is a particular kind of heartbreak that comes not from an enemy's attack, but from the collapse of a foundation you once believed was unshakable. The justice system is meant to be that foundation, an impartial guardian, standing above personal interests, ensuring fairness and protection for all. To discover that this system has failed you is not merely disappointing; it is disorienting, humiliating, and deeply wounding. It is shameful, not because the victim has done wrong, but because the betrayal forces them to bear an undeserved weight of guilt and self-doubt.

The Personal Impact of Betrayal

When you place trust in a system designed to uphold your rights, you are, in essence, surrendering your vulnerability in exchange for protection. The betrayal of that trust can leave lasting scars. It is not just the injustice of the outcome, it is the corrosion of a belief that once gave you a sense of safety. You begin to question your own judgment: Was I naïve to trust? Did I misread the moral fabric of my society? This self-questioning compounds the pain, making it not only a legal defeat but also a deeply personal rupture.

The shame arises from the illusion being shattered in public view. The justice system claims to operate under principles of truth and fairness; when it instead delivers bias, negligence, or corruption, the victim is left exposed to both harm and societal scrutiny. People may quietly, or openly, wonder what you did to "deserve" such treatment. Even without explicit blame, the human mind internalizes the stigma.

The Social Consequences

A justice system that fails individuals does more than harm them personally; it erodes the social fabric. When one person's trust is broken, others begin to doubt. The damage spreads beyond the initial betrayal, planting seeds of cynicism and fear. Communities lose faith in the very mechanisms designed to keep peace. In such a climate, laws may still exist on paper, but the moral authority that gives them legitimacy begins to crumble.

This is not an abstract concern, it has real consequences. People who no longer believe the system will protect them may stop reporting crimes, stop cooperating with authorities, or seek justice outside lawful channels. The spiral of distrust deepens, weakening the rule of law and emboldening those who exploit it for personal gain.

The Psychological Weight of Disillusionment

Perhaps the most painful part of this betrayal is the sense of isolation it brings. When the justice system fails you, it can feel as if the entire society has turned away. Your struggle is no longer just about the original wrong done to you, it becomes a fight against an entrenched institution that refuses to acknowledge its own failings. This leaves you battling both the injustice and the perception that you are powerless against it.

The shame is amplified by the knowledge that, in theory, the system was designed for your protection. You were not wrong to expect fairness; society itself promised it to you. That promise was broken, and in its place lies a silence that feels complicit.

The Need for Accountability

To move beyond shame, there must be both acknowledgment and reform. A justice system that betrays its citizens cannot be left untouched; the moral health of a society depends on holding it accountable. This involves transparency, independent oversight, and a willingness to admit error. Most importantly, it requires listening to those who have been failed, not as nuisances to be managed, but as voices essential to truth and repair.

Conclusion

To feel betrayed by the justice system is to experience a double wound: the harm of the original injustice and the collapse of the trust that was supposed to shield you from it. The shame, while misplaced on the victim's shoulders, is real, because it reflects a deep human need for faith in fairness. If that faith dies, what remains is not merely a personal loss, but a societal crisis.

In the end, shame should not belong to the betrayed, but to the system and those who allow its failings to persist. Yet until that shift happens, the wound remains, a quiet, persistent reminder that the laws written to protect us are only as strong as the justice we are willing to demand.

Chapter Ten

Plead Guilty

Knowing I was wrongfully targeted, I still felt compelled to accept the plea bargain. The threats of continued investigation loomed over me, with the prosecutor warning that failing to comply could lead to unfounded charges of money laundering linked to Ethiopia. I was sending money to Ethiopia for a project I started via CITI Bank; I did not see anything wrong with that. I sent the money via the bank, and somehow, they discovered the transaction. If I was doing it through other means, they would not have found out. Despite all my transactions being legal, the pressure was relentless.

In a way, I entered the plea bargain because I was tired, sick with a minor stroke (TIA), my capacity to think was not strong, the loss of a husband, and their misbehavior of going around to my tenants, friends, and more made me accept the plea bargain hoping that they leave me alone. The harassment was unbearable. I was truly scared to live in my house with my daughter by myself. I did not want them to come at night time to kill us both. I was so scared due to the arrogant behavior displayed by the prosecutor. He was young and inexperienced, he wanted to make a name by winning, and therefore, he did not bother to show courtesy of ethics. He was simply arrogant with zero class with high savage-like behaviors.

In some circumstances, plea bargains result in the loss of trial rights. Defendants give up their right to a jury trial and the chance to be found not guilty, and they usually forfeit the right to appeal once a plea bargain is accepted.

Sometimes, the government initiates a case, abuses the defendant, finds no valid legal violations, and then offers a plea bargain to avoid future liabilities for wrongdoing. There have been documented cases where the government has pursued charges against individuals, only to offer a plea bargain later when their case weakens—often to cover up misconduct or avoid civil liability.

When prosecutors or law enforcement officials engage in misconduct, such as illegal searches, coercion, or the presentation of false evidence, they sometimes offer a plea deal to avoid a full trial where their actions might be exposed. Defendants, even those who are innocent, may accept plea deals out of fear of facing harsher penalties if they go to trial.

One of the most well-known cases of wrongful prosecution and plea deals is the Central Park Five case from 1989. Five teenagers were coerced into false confessions and wrongfully convicted. They accepted plea deals and lesser charges under extreme pressure. Years later, DNA evidence proved their innocence, and the government ultimately paid a $41 million settlement for wrongful prosecution. Another example is the Khalid Awan case in 2006. A Canadian citizen was detained and reportedly tortured by the agency that was involved with that case. He accepted a plea deal on lesser charges, but allegations surfaced that this was merely a cover-up for misconduct during his detention.

When agency misconduct is exposed, wrongful convictions and plea bargains often lead to civil lawsuits. The Chicago Police Torture Scandal is a glaring example, where dozens of individuals were coerced into plea bargains after being physically abused by police. The city ultimately paid out millions in settlements. Similarly, the Baltimore Gun Trace Task Force scandal of the 2010s revealed corrupt police officers planting evidence and pressuring defendants into plea bargains. Once exposed, wrongful convictions were overturned, highlighting the extent to which abuse of power can distort justice.

Legal precedents further demonstrate how plea bargains have been manipulated. In Brady v. Maryland (1963), the Supreme Court ruled that prosecutors must turn over exculpatory evidence to defendants. However, many plea bargains have later been overturned due to violations of this rule. In United States v. Ruiz (2002), the Court ruled that prosecutors are not required to disclose all impeachment evidence before a plea bargain, effectively making it easier for the government to conceal misconduct.

Legal experts and civil rights organizations argue that plea bargains can be abused, particularly when defendants lack the resources to fight wrongful charges. Some states have begun limiting the use of plea bargains in cases where there are allegations of police misconduct. Unfortunately, most ordinary citizens are not equipped or educated enough to understand the complexities of the legal system in this country. This lack of knowledge makes it difficult to make the right decisions in times of crisis, leaving many vulnerable to legal manipulation and coercion.

Hearing such allegations from a supposed protector of justice was beyond belief. These inexperienced agents seemed more interested in scoring victories to inflate their egos than in pursuing truth and justice. Their focus was on meeting quotas and appearing productive, all at the expense of the justice system's integrity.

Their arrogance and disregard for American values clarified that they cared little for justice. They were more concerned with maintaining power and prestige than with the realities of my case. The entire process felt like a farce, a cruel joke played on the very citizens they were supposed to protect. The racist system does not have any value to minorities and black citizens. They are quick to accuse and shoot above their hips without a deep understanding of the case, the allegations, and the fabrication.

Again, no need to investigate a citizen for five years and then blame it on tax returns is truly unbelievable. I am a black woman and an easy target to be accused without following the correct procedure. If the issue and the problem were taxes, to begin with, they would have audited my book. The whole thing does not make any sense. Therefore, I am still searching for the cause of the harassment and the five-year investigation. Maybe black people in this country are not supposed to succeed. As a black person, our success is always under question because of racism in this country. I know all Americans are not racist and yet we have some as interrupters of citizen's lives.

It does not matter how many hurdles we overcome, how hard we work, or how much we contribute—our legitimacy is constantly challenged and our intelligence and caliber are always under question marks. If we succeed, it is assumed we cheated the system. If we fail, it is deemed inevitable. Racism does not allow us the luxury of simply existing and achieving without scrutiny. There is always an assumption that we do not belong, that our presence in spaces of success must be justified and that our victories are anomalies rather than the result of talent and perseverance.

This is not just my story—it is the story of countless black Americans who have built businesses, obtained higher education, and reached positions of influence, only to be met with suspicion, hostility, and attempts to delegitimize their accomplishments. From financial audits to legal entrapments, from racial profiling to workplace discrimination, the barriers are ever-present. When are we going to become worthy citizens?

Even within corporate America, black professionals experience being overlooked for promotions, paid less than their white counterparts, and dismissed as diversity hires instead of being recognized for their qualifications. Black entrepreneurs are questioned about the legitimacy of their businesses, subjected to unnecessary financial scrutiny, and denied access to loans that others receive with ease. The message is clear: our success is always conditional, always questioned.

But racism affects not only Black Americans but also white Americans. Overall, Americans are inherently good-natured, but a small number spread division, hate, and injustice. This small group weaponizes racial biases to maintain power, turning people against one another and distorting the ideals that America claims to stand for. By sowing distrust between races, they weaken the very foundation of a nation built on diversity and opportunity.

For white Americans, the effects of racism can be seen in the erosion of trust, the economic disparities that impact working-class communities, and the growing divide that keeps people from seeing the real enemy—not each other, but the systems that perpetuate injustice. Racism is a tool of control, a means to keep the majority distracted while those in power continue to exploit the vulnerable. It benefits only the elite, not the common citizen. Therefore, black or white, we all are in the same boat.

Many white Americans do not realize how racism has also been used against them. The same system that criminalizes black success also exploits white labor, ensuring that poor and working-class whites remain in economic distress. Instead of recognizing that the real struggle is against corporate greed, corruption, and the erosion of democratic values, they are fed a false narrative that black people are their competition, their enemy. This keeps divisions alive and well, preventing unity that could challenge the real forces of oppression.

Despite all of this, I still believe in the fundamental goodness of people. I have met white Americans who stood up for me, who saw through the injustice and offered their support. There are many who fight for equality, who understand that justice is not about race but about fairness, dignity, and truth. If we as a society could move beyond racial divisions and recognize our shared struggles, we could create a nation that truly upholds its ideals.

The fight against racism is not just a black fight. It is a fight for America's soul. Because when justice is denied to one group, it is eventually denied to all. The question is, *how long will we allow it to continue? How long will we let racism dictate the course of lives, destroy futures, and erode the very freedoms this country was built upon?*

Even as I signed the plea bargain, I knew I was innocent. But innocence means nothing when you are black in America. The plea was not an admission of guilt, it was an act of survival. And that is what racism does. It forces us to make impossible choices just to keep our heads above water.

I did not lose because I was guilty. I lost because I was black. After all, I was successful because I dared to exist in a world that was never meant to accommodate people like me. But I refuse to let them break me. They can take my money, my reputation, and my time, but they *cannot take my voice*. And I will use it to speak against the injustices that have been allowed to thrive for far too long.

I Refuse to Be Silenced

There are moments in life when the weight of injustice feels almost unbearable, when people try to strip you of your dignity, your truth, and your will to stand. I have lived such a moment. I have felt the cold force of others trying to diminish me, to twist my story, to make me small. But I stand here, unbroken.

I refuse to let them break me. They may have tried to crush my spirit, but they cannot take away the fire within me. My voice is mine, born of my truth, shaped by my pain, and strengthened by my survival. No matter how much they want my silence, I will not give it to them.

The injustice I endured was real. It cut deep. It tried to convince me that I was powerless. But power is not always in fists or control over others, it is in the courage to speak when someone has told you to be quiet. And so, I will talk.

I will speak for the truth they tried to bury.

I will speak for the dignity they tried to take.

I will speak for the justice I deserve, and for the justice still denied to so many others.

They wanted my silence because silence protects the powerful. But I have learned that my voice is my weapon, my shield, and my light. Even if it shakes, even if it cracks, it will still be heard.

I am not defined by what was done to me. I am represented by my refusal to surrender, my decision to rise, and my unshakable promise to myself: I will use my voice to speak against the injustice I endured, again, and again, and again, until it can no longer be ignored.

Chapter Eleven
The Good Judge

In the labyrinth of injustice I had been forced to navigate, one beacon of fairness emerged, the good judge. Amid the chaos of coercion, threats, and a legal system that seemed more intent on crushing me than seeking the truth, she stood as a rare symbol of integrity. From the moment she presided over my case, she exuded a presence that commanded respect, not through fear or arrogance, but through an unwavering commitment to justice.

I will never forget how she looked at me, not as a faceless defendant but as a person. While others in the courtroom had already decided my fate, eager to push forward their agendas, she sought understanding. Time and again, she asked me if I was being coerced into accepting the plea bargain. She repeated the question as if she could see past the legal proceedings into the quiet torment that lay beneath. I wanted to tell her. ***I wanted to scream that***, *yes*, I was being forced, manipulated, and threatened into submission. But fear clamped down on my voice. *Honestly, I was tired. I wanted this case to close quickly to travel to my homeland to visit a sick family member and regain myself back from fatigue and harassment.*

The weight of the prosecutor's threats loomed over me like a storm cloud. If I rejected the plea, they would find more ways to punish me, fabricate more charges, and drag me deeper into their web. The uncertainty of what they could do next was suffocating. So, I remained silent. I nodded, signed the papers, and accepted the verdict that was never truly mine to choose.

Yet, the judge did not accept the case at face value. She saw through the facade the injustice thinly veiled beneath layers of legal jargon. Her fairness and diligence reminded me that not everyone in the justice system was driven by ambition or power. Unlike the prosecutor, who was more concerned with his win record than the truth—she held herself to a higher standard. She did not wield her authority recklessly, nor did she let the influence of government pressure dictate her judgment.

Her decision on my sentencing spoke volumes. Instead of allowing the prosecutor to dictate the final blow, she ruled in a way that exposed the absurdity of the entire case. A $50,000 fine was to be paid at $100 per month—without interest. The message was clear: this was not justice, this was a prolonged act of harassment. Her ruling put them in their place, subtly rebuking the wasted years and resources spent vilifying me.

But she did not stop there. She urged the prosecutor and his team to reflect on their actions and to report back to their superiors that this case was riddled with fundamental flaws. She did what she could within the confines of her position—offering me dignity where others had stripped it away. As I left the courtroom, her final words stayed with me.

"Good luck," she said.

Two simple words, yet they carried a weight of genuine goodwill. It was not the cold, detached farewell of a judge who had moved on to the next case. It was an acknowledgment—a silent understanding that I had been wronged, that she saw what others refused to see. In that moment, she restored a small part of the faith I had lost.

Not all within the justice system were corrupt. Not all had been blinded by power. The good judge was proof of that. In the darkest of moments, when everything seems stacked against you, there is often one person who offers a glimmer of hope. It may not be enough to undo the harm that has been inflicted, but it is enough to remind you that fairness still exists in some corners of the world. For me, that person was this judge. She was not obligated to care. She could have simply done what was expected of her, moving on to the next case without a second thought. But she chose to listen, to see me as more than a case file, and to act with integrity when so many others had not.

Her actions did something I had thought impossible: they rekindled a small measure of my faith in America. When I left Ethiopia, I had done so with hope. I believed in the promise of America, a land of justice, opportunity, and freedom. I sacrificed everything to come here, believing that my future would be secure in a country built on the principles of fairness and equality. But my experience with the justice system shattered those ideals. I had seen firsthand how the system could be manipulated, how truth could be discarded, and how the powerful could crush those who lacked the energy to fight back.

Yet, in that courtroom, through the presence of one fair judge, I was reminded that America was not entirely lost. The values I had once admired still existed in some individuals. The country I had believed in was still there, if only in small, isolated moments.

My own case, while not one of wrongful imprisonment, followed the same insidious pattern. The agency's tactics were clear: intimidation, manipulation, and coercion. They used their power to crush me, just as they did with countless others before me.

At this moment, I think of Sallie Taylor, a 63-year-old grandmother in Washington, D.C., whose life was shattered in an instant. One evening in 2015, she sat in the comfort of her home, watching "Bible Talk," when her world was turned upside down.

Without warning, nine heavily armed D.C. police officers stormed through her door, weapons drawn, and pointed a shotgun at her face. They ordered her to the floor as if she were a criminal, as if she were dangerous as if her existence was a threat. But she was just an elderly woman, someone who had never even received a speeding ticket, let alone engaged in any wrongdoing.

The justification for this violent intrusion? A woman, arrested two miles away the night before for possessing a half-ounce vial of PCP, was somehow linked to Sallie Taylor's address—though there was no real evidence of that connection. Taylor had never met this woman, had no involvement in any crime, and yet, for 30 minutes, officers rifled through her belongings, rummaging through her personal items, even violating her privacy by searching her underwear drawer. When they found nothing, they left. No apology. No acknowledgment of their mistake. No accountability for the trauma they had just inflicted upon her.

I think about her fear, about the helplessness that must have overtaken her as she lay there, forced to comply with men who saw her as nothing more than an obstacle in their pursuit of a hollow victory. Somehow, I relate her to myself. I understand her pain, her fear. I sympathize with her. And I think about the lasting impact of that night, how it must have changed the way she saw her home, her country, her place in this world. Just like me, she had been treated as guilty before ever being given a chance to prove her innocence. Just like me, she was a Black woman in America, where justice is too often a privilege, not a right.

Sallie Taylor's experience is not an isolated case. It is part of a long, painful history of wrongful accusations, unjust convictions, and the reckless abuse of power by those sworn to protect. Across the country, people like her—and people like me—suffer under a system that prioritizes wins over truth, aggression over fairness, and power over justice.

I think about the men who spent decades behind bars before finally having their wrongful convictions overturned. Five innocent men in Washington, D.C., had their lives stolen, their futures erased, all because the system refused to admit its mistakes until it was too late. The government eventually established a Conviction Integrity Unit, a team dedicated to reviewing wrongful convictions and attempting to right some of these devastating wrongs. But I ask myself—how many more people remain locked away, lost in the system, their innocence buried under legal bureaucracy? How many more Sallie Taylors will be traumatized in their own homes, their dignity stripped away, without a single consequence for those responsible?

Even the so-called solutions feel inadequate. The Conviction Integrity Unit was a step in the right direction, but it came only after years of destruction had already been done. It was not created because the system cared about justice, but because the system was forced to acknowledge its failures after decades of wrongful imprisonment and public outrage. How many cases will never be reviewed? How many innocent people will never be heard? How many more will be told to accept their fate, to plead guilty simply because fighting back is too exhausting, too costly, too dangerous?

Sallie Taylor's story reminds me of my own. It reminds me that this system does not wait for proof before deciding who is guilty. It does not require real evidence to justify ripping someone's life apart. It only requires a target, and once that target is chosen, justice no longer matters. Her home was violated just as my life was, her dignity discarded just as mine was, her innocence presumed irrelevant—just as mine was.

And so I ask again: how many more?

This experience left me with lessons that will remain with me forever. I now know that justice is not guaranteed—it must be fought for, understood, and protected. I urge every law-abiding citizen to educate themselves about the legal system. Knowledge is the only shield against those who would abuse their power. Had I known then what I know now, perhaps I would have spoken up. Perhaps I would have found the courage to tell the judge what she already suspected: that I had been forced into a plea I never should have accepted.

But fear is a powerful thing. It silences the innocent and emboldens the corrupt. It keeps justice just out of reach.

Yet, within that courtroom, despite all that had transpired, the judge had offered me something I had not encountered for years in this battle—a measure of fairness, a glimpse of what justice was meant to be.

She was not the system; she was the exception to it. She was the beacon of light that helped restore my faith in America, even if only a little. And for that, I will always be grateful.

Etifework Gebre Wold, Zed's mother.

Wondemu Belaynehe, Zed's father.

Chapter Twelve
Trailblazers

The United States of America is a nation built on the dreams, struggles, and triumphs of immigrants and natives who have worked tirelessly to create a land of opportunity. The strength of this nation lies in its people—their perseverance, innovation, and determination to overcome adversity. From the earliest Indigenous communities to the waves of immigrants who sought a better future, the spirit of hard work has been the cornerstone of American success. Together, they have shaped industries, advanced technologies, and enriched the country's cultural fabric, making the United States a beacon of hope and progress.

Long before the arrival of European settlers, Native American communities flourish across the vast expanse of what is now the United States. They cultivated the land, built intricate societies, and developed sustainable living methods that balanced progress with nature. Tribes such as the Iroquois, Cherokee, and Navajo created governance systems, intricate trade networks, and art forms that continue to influence modern America. Their resilience in the face of hardship is a testament to the enduring strength of the human spirit.

Despite historical challenges, Native Americans have contributed to the nation's growth. Many Indigenous leaders and entrepreneurs have emerged as key figures in agriculture, education, and environmental conservation. Their unwavering connection to the land has played a vital role in preserving natural resources and advocating for sustainable development, ensuring that future generations inherit a world that values both progress and tradition.

The contributions of African Americans and Black immigrants to the United States are immeasurable. From the forced arrival of enslaved Africans to the waves of voluntary immigration from the Caribbean, Africa, and other parts of the world, Black communities have played an essential role in shaping the nation's economy, culture, and social progress.

Enslaved Africans were instrumental in building the agricultural economy of the South, working tirelessly on plantations that produced cotton, tobacco, and sugar—key exports that fueled America's early growth. Despite the oppressive system of slavery, Black Americans resisted, innovated, and laid the foundation for future generations to thrive. Figures such as Frederick Douglass, Harriet Tubman, and Sojourner Truth fought for freedom and justice, helping to reshape the nation's moral and political landscape.

In the aftermath of slavery, African Americans continued to push forward, making strides in education, business, and civil rights. The Great Migration saw millions move from the South to northern and western cities, seeking better opportunities and contributing to industrial growth. Leaders like Booker T. Washington and W.E.B. Du Bois advocated for education and equality, while Black entrepreneurs such as Madam C.J. Walker built successful enterprises that uplifted communities.

Black immigrants have also played a significant role in America's progress. Caribbean and African immigrants have contributed immensely to medicine, technology, and the arts. Figures such as Marcus Garvey, Shirley Chisholm, and contemporary business leaders have shaped political movements and industries, furthering the legacy of Black excellence and resilience.

Immigrants have always been at the heart of America's development, bringing diverse skills, perspectives, and an unyielding work ethic. From the earliest European settlers to modern-day newcomers, immigrants have sought to build better lives for themselves and the generations that follow. Their willingness to embrace challenges and adapt to new environments has fueled the country's economic and social progress.

The Industrial Revolution saw an influx of immigrants from Ireland, Italy, Germany, and Eastern Europe, as well as African Americans who worked in factories, railroads, and mines, laying the groundwork for America's rise as an industrial power. Chinese immigrants were crucial in constructing the Transcontinental Railroad, while Mexican laborers contributed significantly to the agricultural sector. The sacrifices of these individuals were instrumental in transforming the United States into an economic powerhouse.

Immigrants continue to drive innovation and progress across various sectors, including technology, medicine, and entrepreneurship. Many of the world's leading companies, such as Google, Tesla, and Apple, have been founded or led by immigrants or their descendants. Their success stories reflect the values of perseverance and hard work that define the American Dream.

What unites both immigrants and natives is their shared spirit of resilience and determination. This unwavering commitment to hard work has driven America's progress, enabling the country to overcome economic crises, technological shifts, and global challenges. The ability to adapt, innovate, and collaborate has ensured that the United States remains a leader on the world stage.

Communities across the country demonstrate this tenacity every day. Whether farmers cultivate the land, construction workers build infrastructure, or scientists develop groundbreaking medical treatments, the contributions of both immigrants and natives shape the nation's future. The shared belief in the value of hard work fosters unity and strengthens the fabric of American society.

As America continues to evolve, embracing diversity and inclusion remains essential. By acknowledging and celebrating the contributions of both immigrants and native-born citizens, the nation can move forward with a collective sense of purpose. Policies that promote equal opportunities, education, and economic mobility will ensure that all individuals, regardless of their background, have the chance to succeed. The right direction for America is not in demoralizing or undervaluing its immigrants but in recognizing their intelligence and contributions. All people, regardless of color or creed, are born with talents, and undermining immigrant intelligence is a failure to acknowledge reality.

The challenges of the modern era require an innovative, adaptable, and diverse workforce. By investing in the talents and skills of all people, America can continue to be a land of opportunity where hard work is rewarded and dreams become reality. The strength of this nation lies not in division but in unity—where immigrants and natives work side by side to build a brighter future.

The United States is a testament to the power of resilience, determination, and collaboration. Both immigrants and natives have played indispensable roles in shaping the country's identity, proving that success is achieved through perseverance and a strong work ethic. As the nation continues to grow and evolve, this shared spirit of hard work will propel America toward an even greater future. By recognizing the contributions of all who call this land home, the United States can remain a beacon of hope, prosperity, and opportunity for future generations. Truthfully recording all accomplishments and ensuring justice for all is the way forward.

Dr. Basliel Wolde Gabriel, Zed's late husband.

Retrospective

Looking back, I find myself overwhelmed by the weight of regret. There are moments I wish I could revisit—not to change the past, but to give my former self the clarity, strength, and guidance I so desperately needed at the time. The decisions I made, though well-intentioned, have left lingering questions in my heart.

First and foremost, I wish I had not cooperated with the plea bargain. At the time, I believed I was doing the right thing by being cooperative and transparent. I believed that honesty would prevail, that truth would protect me. Instead, I found myself trapped in a system that did not honor my integrity. I felt like I was penalized not for wrongdoing, but for placing my faith in a process that ultimately failed me.

I also wish I had not agreed to extend the investigation period. I did so with the belief that it would demonstrate my sincerity and innocence. I thought that by allowing more time, I was showing I had nothing to hide. I had built a life based on hard work, resilience, and the pursuit of the American dream. I never imagined that my dedication and diligence would be met with suspicion rather than appreciation. The extension, intended to display good faith, only prolonged the emotional toll and left me caught in an endless storm of uncertainty.

Another decision I regret is not taking my story to the media. I remained silent, hoping that if I kept my head down, everything would eventually go away. I believed that disappearing quietly was the best way to preserve what little peace I had left. But in doing so, I gave up my voice. I let others tell my story—or worse, allowed it to go untold. If I had come forward publicly, perhaps the truth would have found more light, and others in similar situations might have found courage through my experience.

I also deeply regret not reaching out to my community and friends. I carried the burden alone, isolated by fear, shame, and confusion. I assumed they wouldn't understand, or that I would be judged. But now I realize how powerful it would have been to speak up—to invite support, to lean on those who cared for me, to let them walk with me through that darkness. Isolation only deepened my pain.

Compounding all of this was my health. I suffered a minor stroke (a transient ischemic attack, or TIA) during that time, which impaired my thinking and weakened my ability to respond with the clarity and focus I normally possess. That moment of vulnerability left me defenseless at a time when I needed to be at my sharpest. I often wonder what might have been different if my body had not failed me.

I was also utterly exhausted—physically, emotionally, and financially. I had poured so much of myself into surviving, into fighting for what I believed was right, that there was nothing left. I was running on empty. The shadow of defeat followed me closely; I was sick and tired in every sense of the word. It's difficult to navigate a battle when you no longer have the strength to lift your shield.

In hindsight, I see how much my silence cost me. I see how the choices I made out of trust, fear, or fatigue led to outcomes I never intended. And while I cannot rewrite history, I can share these reflections in the hope that they might guide someone else, somewhere, to make a different choice—to speak up, to stand tall, to seek help, to believe in their worth, even when the world seems to crumble around them.

This is my truth. This is my retrospective. A message not just of regret, but of resilience—because even in pain, there is the possibility of healing, of learning, and of becoming whole again.

Lessons for My Children

Do not be afraid to go into business because of my experience.

In America, small businesses have long been the backbone of the economy, a pillar of prosperity and innovation. They represent the beating heart of our free-market system, which is built not just on capital but on the courage, creativity, and persistence of everyday individuals. These businesses embody the American Dream: the idea that with vision, hard work, and perseverance, anyone can build something lasting and meaningful. They are living proof that the spirit of enterprise is alive and well in this great nation.

Every large corporation we see today—Apple, Amazon, or Ford—once began as a small idea. They were once nothing more than a person or two with an idea, a garage, and an unshakable belief in what they could create. That is the power of small business. It gives rise to innovation. It allows talent to flourish. It transforms lives—not just between the business owners, but of those they employ and the communities they serve. In doing so, small businesses mightily contribute to the overall health and growth of the U.S. economy.

A Nation Built for Builders

The American system is uniquely suited for entrepreneurs. When functioning as intended, it is an environment that encourages innovation, supports competition, and rewards those willing to take risks. Our institutions, our access to capital, our relatively free markets, and our long-standing culture of entrepreneurialism all serve as fertile soil for new ideas to take root and grow. Unlike many places in the world, America gives people the room to try, to fail, and to try again.

The pathway is not always easy, but it is accessible. For those who have stamina, creativity, grit, and the spirit of hard work, this country offers a rare opportunity: to build something from nothing, to use one's God-given talents and vision to create not only a livelihood but also a legacy. The fruits of entrepreneurship are financial independence, personal fulfillment, and the ability to contribute meaningfully with impact to society.

The Role of Government: Help or Hindrance?

However, this journey can be made easier or harder depending on the environment set by those in power. Pro-business leadership—those who understand the value of free enterprise and seek to foster a supportive ecosystem—can propel innovation and unleash a wave of creative productivity. On the other hand, overregulation, bureaucracy, and policies that stifle rather than stimulate can hinder the small business community and discourage potential entrepreneurs from trying.

It's not about favoring the rich or abandoning necessary safeguards. It's about balance. When government policies become too controlling, too restrictive, or too discouraging, they can smother the very thing that has made America strong: the willingness of individuals to take risks, innovate, and build. A healthy economy is not created by handouts or red tape—it is driven by people with ideas and the freedom to pursue them.

When America has the right government—one that respects the importance of small businesses and fosters the conditions in which creativity can thrive—there is no limit to what can be achieved. We must remain vigilant in protecting that spirit and ensuring that our laws and policies empower rather than suppress the entrepreneurial drive that defines our nation.

A Word to the Next Generation

To my children and anyone reading this who may be hesitant to take that first step: do not be afraid to start your own business. Do not be discouraged by my frustrations or experiences with specific government sectors. The entrepreneurship journey is filled with challenges, but it is also rich with rewards. You are not limited by what has happened to others; you are empowered by your own talents, passions, and potential.

Use your creativity. Trust your instincts. Lean on your faith, your work ethic, and your resilience. Build something with your own hands, even if it starts small. You do not need to wait for permission. You do not need to follow someone else's script. This country was made for builders, dreamers, and doers.

Financial independence is not just about money; it's about freedom. It's about self-respect. It's about supporting yourself, your family, and your community in a way that honors your gifts and values. And when more citizens achieve that independence, our nation is more substantial. We have become less dependent on the government, more engaged with one another, and more confident in our future.

Conclusion

In closing, let us remember that America's greatness has always been rooted in its people—their ambition, dreams, and courage to take chances. Small businesses are not just economic units. They are expressions of freedom, engines of innovation, and are essential to the health and future of this country.

Let us continue to protect and promote that spirit. Let us inspire the next generation to create, to lead, and to never be afraid of building something beautiful—no matter how small it starts. In

America, with the right heart and effort, even the smallest idea can become something world-changing. Less government harassment helps a great deal to financial independence and community empowerment.

Know your rights and educate yourself to learn more about the legal system. If you are aware of the legal system, you can be the perfect defender of yourself.

Have time to research and hire the best lawyer. All lawyers are not the same.

Do not hate anyone regardless; always be a peacemaker. Strive to love, and to do good. Avoid hate as hate kills you first before it reaches anyone. Do not hate anyone. Honey is better than vinegar. When you love, you will be the happiest person on this earth. Hate destroys the hater first. Do not hate anyone. Respect all people; do not forgo your value when encountering haters, trouble makers, and slackers. Do not allow anyone to make you lose your value and standard. Do not scoop down to your enemies level. ***Do-not-go-low.*** Always stay confident. If possible, teach the right thing to your enemy if they are willing to learn.

Challenges and struggles make you a better person. Try to understand the issue behind the challenge. Sometimes, one becomes a target because of the timing. In my case, it seemed September 11 made a few people angry.

Do not allow obstacles to change you as a human. Always depend on yourself and the supreme power you worship. For some, it is God; for some, it is Allah, etc.

Always connect and worship in times of difficulty. Know that as much as some people are mean, there are more kind and compassionate people on this earth, so unite and identify yourself with good-doers. Do not give up. Perseverance, persistence, and hard work always pay off. Somehow, someday justice will prevail.

Have a love for humanity and your country. Always be fair and apply justice in all your dealings, whether personal or professional.

Fight, fight for the right thing and justice.

When you see injustice, fight it. You are a dead wood if you do not stop your neighbor's injustice. Always try to be truthful to yourself and others. Do not go with the flow. Be a good friend, a good neighbor, a good worker, and a good citizen to create your happiness. Do not cheat anyone, always be truthful. Those who think they can outsmart you by telling you untruthful stories will pay the price. Plus, they lose your respect. My children - be strong financially, emotionally, and spiritually. Be a giver not a taker as giving and sharing brings blessings in your life. Always, stand for the right thing. Avoid haters and bullies. Again, respect all people and try to be a good example even at times you have to pay an emotional price. Do not allow anyone to let you lose your inner peace. The peace that you only receive from your God, your Creator. Let them eat their heart out as long as God is on your side.

Be human not a robot or a machine!

Zed with her children and husband.

Zed's mother, Etifework Gebre Wold, when she was young.

Retrospective Reflections

Looking back, there are several actions I would reconsider:

- *Plea Bargain:* In hindsight, I regret agreeing to the plea bargain.

- *Extended Investigation:* Despite my transparency and honesty, extending the investigation period only prolonged an ordeal I never deserved. My only intention was to demonstrate my integrity, as I had done nothing but work diligently to pursue the American dream.

- *Public Awareness:* I wish I had shared my story with the media early on, rather than hoping it would fade away in silence.

- *Community and Support:* I regret not keeping my community and friends informed about my struggles during that time.

- *Health Challenge:* A minor stroke (TIA) affected my judgment and resilience. Had I been in better health, I believe I could have responded more effectively.

- *Confidence and Self-Assurance:* I wish I had found a way to shield myself from the damage to my self-confidence throughout the process.

Afterword

I wrote this book to express my disappointment and frustration with a system that, instead of rewarding hard work and integrity, seems to penalize it. Despite dedicating myself to honest labor and following every rule, I found myself targeted by a system that lets true criminals roam freely while it chooses to harass a hardworking citizen like me based on false information and baseless allegations.

This book is also for others who have suffered similar injustices—those who, like me, have felt disillusioned by a legal system that should protect us but instead threatens our stability. I want people who have faced these challenges to find solace in knowing they are not alone. By sharing our experiences, we can gain strength from each other, raise our voices, and work toward a fairer system. This country is as much ours as anyone's, and we have every right to demand fair treatment and justice.

Those who come after us should know that they may face trials not because they are wrong, but because they are resilient, hardworking, ***independent thinkers*** who cannot be controlled. Why should my growth, my finances, or my lifestyle be questioned when I have achieved everything through my own diligence and ability? "What is good for the goose is good for the gander." Do not allow anyone to make you feel you are not entitled to a good life.

My experiences have shown me how easily some people in power can misuse their authority to destroy a life based on limited, biased information. I think back to a story I saw on the news about a young Black man who was interrogated by the police while simply washing his dog. The dog was crying and it was mistaken for a beating. A young neighbor reported him and without a thorough investigation, the police took action against him. The tragedy of such events strikes at the heart of what America stands for. This is a great nation, founded on principles meant to protect us all. We have rights here—the very Bill of Rights guarantees them.

The Bill of Rights was introduced to limit government power and protect individual freedoms. Yet, my experience reveals a system that often ignores the principles these amendments represent. These amendments—protecting speech, privacy, due process, and fair trials—form the foundation of American liberty. I include them here to remind readers of these basic protections that should stand between us and misuse of power.

The U.S. Constitution, adopted on September 17, 1787, is the foundational legal document of the United States. It established the framework for the national government and is one of the world's oldest constitutions still in use. The Constitution consists of the following main parts:

1. **Preamble**

- The Preamble introduces the Constitution and outlines the purpose of the document, beginning with the famous words, "We the People." It declares the intent to form a more perfect union, establish justice, ensure domestic tranquility, provide for the common defense, promote the general welfare, and secure the blessings of liberty.

2. **Articles (7 Articles)**

- The Constitution is organized into seven articles, each addressing a specific function or principle of government.

- **Article I: The Legislative Branch**
    - Establishes Congress, which is responsible for making laws. Congress is bicameral, consisting of the House

- Details the powers and limitations of Congress, including taxation, defense, and interstate commerce.

- **Article II: The Executive Branch**

  - Establishes the presidency and the executive branch, which is responsible for enforcing laws.

  - Defines the powers of the president, including serving as the commander-in-chief, negotiating treaties, and appointing officials (with Senate approval).

- **Article III: The Judicial Branch**

  - Establishes the Supreme Court and authorizes Congress to create lower courts.

  - Defines the jurisdiction of the courts and outlines the process of judicial review (implied and later confirmed in Marbury v. Madison).

- **Article IV: States' Powers and Limits**

  - Addresses the relationship between the states and the federal government.

  - Guarantees a republican form of government for each state and provides for mutual respect for state laws, as well as admission of new states.

- **Article V: The Amendment Process**

  - Describes the process for amending the Constitution, allowing changes through a formal proposal by two-thirds of Congress or a national convention, followed by ratification by three-fourths of the states.

- **Article VI: Federal Power**
  - Establishes the Constitution as the supreme law of the land.
  - Requires an oath of office for federal and state officials and prohibits any religious tests for officeholders.
- **Article VII: Ratification**
  - Specifies that the Constitution would take effect once ratified by nine of the thirteen original states.

3. The Amendments

- The Constitution has been amended 27 times to address issues, clarify rights, and refine governmental procedures. The first ten amendments, known as the **Bill of Rights**, were added in 1791 to ensure individual freedoms and limit government power.
  - **First Amendment:** Freedom of religion, speech, press, assembly, and petition.
  - **Second Amendment:** Right to bear arms.
  - **Thirteenth Amendment:** Abolishment of slavery.
  - **Fourteenth Amendment:** Equal protection under the law and due process.
  - **Nineteenth Amendment:** Women's suffrage.
  - **Twenty-sixth Amendment:** Lowering of the voting age to 18.

Key Principles of the U.S. Constitution

- **Separation of Powers:** Divides government into three branches, each with distinct powers to prevent the concentration of power.

- **Checks and Balances:** Each branch has powers that can counterbalance the others, ensuring cooperation and preventing abuse.

- **Federalism:** Shares power between the national and state governments.

- **Popular Sovereignty:** The government derives its power from the people.

- **Individual Rights:** Protects individual liberties and rights.

The Constitution is brief but profoundly impactful, evolving through amendments and interpretations that have allowed it to remain relevant across centuries.

The **Bill of Rights** is the collective name for the first ten amendments to the **United States Constitution**, ratified on December 15, 1791. These amendments were introduced to protect individual liberties and limit government power, addressing concerns raised during the Constitution's ratification process. Below is a summary of each amendment:

1. **First Amendment**

- Guarantees the freedoms of **speech**, **religion**, **press**, **assembly**, and **petition**.

- Protects individuals' rights to express themselves without government interference.

2. **Second Amendment**

- Protects the right to **keep and bear arms**.

- Originally tied to the idea of a "well-regulated militia," it has since been interpreted to protect personal gun ownership rights.

3. **Third Amendment**

- Prohibits the **quartering of soldiers** in private homes without the owner's consent.

- Reflects concerns from colonial times when British soldiers were often housed in American homes.

4. **Fourth Amendment**

- Protects against **unreasonable searches and seizures**.

- Requires law enforcement to have a warrant, based on probable cause, to conduct searches of property or individuals.

5. **Fifth Amendment**

- Establishes the right to **due process of law** and protection against **double jeopardy** (being tried twice for the same offense) and self-incrimination.

- Includes the principle of **eminent domain**, allowing the government to take private property for public use with fair compensation.

6. **Sixth Amendment**

- Guarantees the right to a **speedy and public trial**, an **impartial jury**, and the right to **confront witnesses**.

- Ensures the accused has the right to a lawyer and to be informed of the charges against them.

7. **Seventh Amendment**

- Provides for the right to a **jury trial in civil** cases involving claims of more than $20 (a considerable amount at the time of writing).

- Emphasizes the importance of a jury's role in civil matters.

8. **Eighth Amendment**

- Prohibits **excessive bail**, **excessive fines**, and **cruel and unusual punishment**.

- Focuses on fairness and humanity in the criminal justice system.

9. **Ninth Amendment**

- Clarifies that the **listing of certain rights** in the Constitution does not mean that other rights held by the people are denied or disparaged.

- Protects "unenumerated" rights, suggesting individuals have other fundamental rights beyond those listed.

10. **Tenth Amendment**

- Affirms that powers not specifically granted to the **federal government** nor prohibited to the **states** by the Constitution are reserved to the states or the people.

- Reinforces the principles of **federalism** and **state sovereignty**.

The **Bill of Rights** serves as a foundational document for American liberty, aiming to protect citizens' freedoms and maintain a balance between individual rights and governmental powers.

When power falls into the wrong hands, unchecked, it can be devastating. There are those who, if they choose, can ruin lives—unconstrained by the Constitution, morality, or common humanity. As someone who has lived this reality, I feel a duty to tell others: be vigilant. When you begin to succeed, not everyone will cheer for you. Some may view your achievements with suspicion or resentment. Stand firm. Don't let anyone distract you or diminish your purpose. Their harassment aims to make you a liability, but you must remain an asset to yourself and your community. Instead of succumbing to bitterness, keep moving forward with purpose and positivity.

When we face setbacks, it's not the end; it's an invitation to rise, to learn, and to understand those who have endured similar challenges. My ordeal has taught me to listen deeply and to empathize in ways I wouldn't have otherwise. I once might not have believed such experiences could happen in America, yet here I am. I hope that, by reading my story, others can find encouragement and affirmation. Even under unfair scrutiny, refuse to let others' misconceptions define you.

Had this injustice occurred in a less-developed country, I might have accepted it as a harsh reality. But this is America. It is heartbreaking to feel betrayed by a system I once trusted, simply for using my gifts, for innovating, and for multiplying the talents I've been given. I know this much: resilience works. And I will continue, undeterred, with faith that perseverance will prevail.

About the Book

Slanted Justice offers a poignant exploration of Zed Wondemu's experiences with systemic inequities as an Ethiopian immigrant in America. Through gripping narratives and personal anecdotes, Zed sheds light on her challenges while navigating a legal system that often seems stacked against marginalized communities.

This powerful book highlights the struggles of individuals confronting injustice, providing a raw and honest account of the obstacles many face in their pursuit of equality.

Acknowledgments

I would like to begin by thanking my Creator, God, for His unwavering protection and guidance, often in ways beyond my understanding. His grace and favor have shaped my life, guiding me toward the destiny and purpose He set for me from the very beginning a plan no one can alter.

To my late mother, Etifework Gebre Wold, and my late father, Wondemu Belaynehe, thank you for raising me with boundless love and a comfortable life. The confidence you placed in me serves as a constant source of strength and resilience, propelling me forward.

To my late husband, Dr. Basliel Gabriel, who entrusted me with the freedom to pursue my passions without restraint or discouragement, thank you. Your unwavering support, especially during my years managing the restaurant, allowed me to fully focus on my work. This book is dedicated to you, with profound love and gratitude.

I am deeply grateful to my children for their cooperation, patience, and kindness. Their love and understanding eased my path, allowing me to devote time to my endeavors. They have been a great source of joy and inspiration, contributing immensely to my success and happiness without demanding anything like regular children. They were born mature.

I am extending my appreciation to my youngest brother, Tamiru Wondemu for being with me at all times, assisting me, driving me to the court, and staying with me in the courtroom. Without him, it would have been more difficult. I thank him for everything. I appreciate his support and his time in times of difficulty. Stay cool.

To my dear friend Alem Woldehawariat Mathis, my rock and anchor thank you for your steadfast support, listening ear, and constant encouragement. Your advice and loyalty have been invaluable, and I am forever grateful for your presence in my life. You are more than a friend; you are a sister and confidant. You are the best! My hat is off for you.

I also extend my heartfelt thanks to Dr. Tsehaye Teferra for his insights, guidance, and support throughout the writing of this book. Your advice and patience have been instrumental and I am grateful for the time advice.

Many thanks to Kidist Ebebezer for critiquing the book cover and redesigning it for me. I appreciate your talent, creativity, and inventiveness. I love the new book cover.

My sincere gratitude goes to the late Dr. Samuel L. Myers, my first mentor in this country, who believed in me and offered me my first professional opportunity in the President's Office when he was the President of Bowie State University. He witnessed my professional growth and supported me unwaveringly. Thank you, Dr. Myers, for lifting me and, in turn, my family. Your example taught me the importance of extending a helping hand to others when possible. You are remembered with great respect and admiration.

My friend, my roommate, Tedjitou Desalege for her advice, support, and encouragement at all times. I appreciate our long-time friendship and sincere relationship based on respect and admiration.

Finally, to my many friends and family members thank you for your encouragement, support, and acceptance. I am blessed to have an incredible network of people who surround me with love and respect. I cherish each of you deeply.

About the Author

Zed Wondemu has served the Washington area in different capacities for over 40 years. She started gift shops and restaurants and used her business to help others gain employment and provide jobs. She mentored and made young people marketable to the Western workforce. Zed enjoys investing her time, resources, and energy in people (investment in humans versus capital investment).

Born in Ethiopia, Zed Wondemu has combined her remarkable drive with a desire to promote/educate the love of her culture (Ethiopian culture) through sharing good food and Ethiopian hospitality. She has become one of DC's most successful foreign-born women restaurateurs. Zed is the "Board Emeriti" of numerous local organizations, including the National Restaurant Association, Restaurant Association of Metro Washington, and National Restaurant Association Education Foundation.

Zed's Ethiopian Restaurant opened in Georgetown in 1988. As owner, president, and manager, Zed presided over a restaurant that had become an area favorite, winning critical acclaim from the Washingtonian as "one of Washington's 100 Very Best Restaurants" for twenty-three years. She was also involved in real estate ventures in the USA, Ethiopia, and Bulgaria. The food and atmosphere were so popular that Zed added a second location in Gainesville, Virginia.

The second Zed's Ethiopian Restaurant opened in January 2009, it became a popular place for lunch and dinner, with catering available at both locations. Zed Wondemu is more cheerful when she helps others; she enjoys philanthropy the most. She has a special heart and mind, observing women succeed in education, politics, and employment. She extends her help to ensure women are the beneficiaries of their dreams.

Zed Wondemu engaged in non-profit organizations (EDG), which provide micro-loans to low- to medium-income individuals to achieve self-sufficiency. Zed Wondemu is a recipient of so many awards, including a recipient of ***The Thomas Carvel Immigrant Entrepreneur Award***. Zed has been profiled in different magazines and newspapers for her work, including "Making it in America/Conversations with Successful Ethiopian American Entrepreneurs."

Currently, she is extending her expertise to those who seek her help to improve their businesses/organizations through her consulting service, Zed's Consulting Services.

www.ingramcontent.com/pod-product-compliance
Lightning Source LLC
Chambersburg PA
CBHW040846120626
46547CB00001B/43